# A Tactical Cookbook for Preppers

## Ancient Methods for Modern Survival



## Noah King

# Table of Contents

# INTRODUCTION

In a period when self-sufficiency and resiliency are highly valued qualities, the art of survival encompasses more than just the provision of food; it also requires an in-depth study of preservation methods that are able to withstand the test of time. Welcome to "A Tactical Cookbook for Preppers: Ancient Methods for Modern Survival."

The importance of being self-sufficient has never been more apparent than it is in the current world, which is fraught with unpredictability. Preppers are equipped with the essential skills necessary to thrive in any condition by reading this book, which acts as a beacon of information and draws from old culinary expertise. The research of time-honored methods of food preservation, such as pickling and fermenting, which have been effective in maintaining civilizations throughout the ages, is at the core of this endeavor.

You are about to go on a journey through the rich tapestry of pickling and fermenting, discovering the science, history, and practical uses of these procedures. This adventure will take place inside these pages. Each chapter is a demonstration of the inventiveness and resourcefulness of the human race in the face of adversity. From the simple beginnings of preserving meals for long voyages to the sophisticated art of constructing gourmet ferments, each chapter is a monument to the human race's ability to overcome challenges.

As you dig deeper into the world of pickling and fermenting, you will discover the mysteries of microbiology. You will discover how beneficial bacteria can turn simple foods into complex flavors and nutritional powerhouses. You will learn about the alchemy of fermentation, which is a process that requires time and care to produce foods that not only make the body healthier but also nourish the spirit.

However, this book is more than just a guide to pickling and fermenting; it is a celebration of the human spirit's ability to persevere, adapt, and overcome adversity. This serves as a timely reminder that in the face of unpredictability, there is strength in possessing knowledge, and that tradition provides nourishment. We invite you to accompany us on a voyage through the annals of culinary history as we investigate the ancient techniques of pickling and fermenting, and uncover the eternal significance of these techniques in the present world. This adventure is open to anyone, whether you are an experienced prepper or a curious novice.

# CHAPTER I

# Understanding Pickling and Fermenting

## Importance of Preservation Techniques in Survival Cooking

The essence of survival cooking is not just in preparing food under constrained circumstances but also in the preservation techniques that ensure sustenance over extended periods. These methods are paramount for survival in adverse conditions, where conventional means of food procurement and preservation are not accessible. Preservation techniques in survival cooking extend the shelf life of food, safeguard nutritional value, and reduce the risk of foodborne illnesses, playing a crucial role in survival scenarios ranging from natural disasters to remote wilderness expeditions.

Food preservation in survival situations relies on methods that do not require modern conveniences such as electricity or sophisticated equipment. Techniques such as drying, smoking, salting, and fermenting have been used for centuries and remain relevant today due to their effectiveness and simplicity. Through the process of drying, which is one of the oldest methods, moisture is removed from food in order to prevent the growth of bacteria. This technique is beneficial for preserving fruits, vegetables, and meats. In survival cooking, the sun, wind, or fire can serve as heat sources for drying, making it an accessible option in various environments.

Smoking, another traditional method, imparts flavor while extending the shelf life of foods, particularly meats and fish. The smoke contains antimicrobial and antioxidant compounds, contributing to preservation. In survival situations, smoking can be accomplished with a simple setup, such as a pit or a makeshift smoker, using available wood. This method preserves food and enhances its palatability, which can be a morale booster in challenging conditions.

Salting is a preservation technique that involves using salt to draw moisture out of food, thereby inhibiting the growth of bacteria, yeast, as well as molds. It is effective for preserving meats and fish and can be combined with drying for added preservation. In survival scenarios, where resources are limited, the ability to keep food with salt—a readily available and transportable resource—can be a lifesaver.

Fermentation is a process that relies on microorganisms which includes bacteria and yeast to convert sugars into alcohol, gases, or organic acids. This transformation preserves the food and enhances its nutritional content and digestibility. Fermented foods which includes sauerkraut, kimchi, and yogurt can provide essential nutrients and probiotics, which are beneficial for gut health. In survival contexts, fermentation can preserve perishable items while boosting nutrition and flavor. These

preservation techniques are practical for extending the shelf life of food and essential for maintaining a balanced diet in survival situations. By preserving various foods, survivors can ensure access to a range of nutrients, which is crucial for health and well-being when fresh produce may be scarce. Furthermore, these methods can help minimize food waste, enabling survivors to make the most of their resources.

The importance of preservation techniques in survival cooking also lies in their role in food safety. Consuming spoiled and/or contaminated food can lead to foodborne illnesses, which can be specifically dangerous in survival situations where medical care may not be readily available. By effectively preserving food, the risk of such diseases is significantly reduced, contributing to the overall safety and success of survival endeavors.

Moreover, the knowledge and skills of these preservation techniques empower individuals to be more self-reliant and prepared for emergencies. Understanding how to preserve food using simple, low-tech methods can make a substantial difference in survival situations, where reliance on conventional food supply chains is not feasible. This knowledge enhances individuals' ability to survive in adverse conditions and fosters a deeper connection with traditional food practices and the natural environment.

In conclusion, the importance of preservation techniques in survival cooking cannot be overstated. These methods play a crucial part in ensuring food security, safety, and nutrition in situations where conventional food procurement and preservation methods are unavailable. By extending the shelf life of food, minimizing the risk of foodborne illnesses, and enabling a diversified diet, preservation techniques are indispensable for survival.

Moreover, the skills and knowledge associated with these methods contribute to self-reliance and resilience, qualities that are invaluable in facing the uncertainties of the natural world. As we continue to navigate the difficulties posed by natural disasters, climate change, and remote exploration, the role of preservation techniques in survival cooking remains more relevant than ever, highlighting the enduring connection between human ingenuity and the quest for sustenance in the face of adversity.

# Historical Background of Pickling and Fermenting

The practices of pickling and fermenting are among the oldest food preservation methods, with a rich history that spans across cultures and continents. These techniques have been pivotal in shaping human diets, enabling societies to store food for longer periods, enhance its flavor, and improve nutritional value. The historical background of pickling and fermenting reveals a culinary evolution and a fascinating intersection of culture, science, and survival.

Pickling, at its core, involves preserving food in an acidic medium, typically vinegar, or through natural fermentation in brine, which leads to an acidic environment. This process not only prolongs the shelf life of foods but also imparts a unique taste and texture. The origins of pickling are believed to date back to ancient Mesopotamia, around 2400 B.C., when cucumbers from India were first pickled. The technique quickly spread to Egypt, where it became a standard method for preserving various foods, including fish and meats, which were essential for sustaining their large workforce, especially during the construction of the pyramids.

The art of fermenting food, which relies on the natural process of lacto-fermentation, has its roots in various ancient cultures. The production of lactic acid is a natural process that occurs when bacteria consume the sugar and starch that are present in the food. This not only preserves the food but also creates beneficial enzymes, b-vitamins, Omega-3 fatty acids, and various strains of probiotics. Historical evidence suggests that as early as 7000 B.C., the Chinese were fermenting cabbage, which would later evolve into what we recognize today as kimchi. Similarly, kefir—a fermented milk drink—dates back over 3,000 years to the pastoral cultures of the Caucasus region, illustrating the widespread adoption and adaptation of fermentation techniques.

The significance of these practices extended beyond mere food preservation. For ancient seafarers and travelers, pickled and fermented foods provided a sustainable source of nutrition during long voyages. Notably, fermented foods like sauerkraut became a vital part of sailors' diets, credited with preventing scurvy, a disease caused by vitamin C deficiency, on long sea voyages. This remarkable discovery highlighted the health benefits of fermented foods, beyond their utility as a preservation method.

The globalization of pickling and fermenting practices can be attributed to trade routes and conquests, which facilitated the exchange of culinary traditions and ingredients. The Romans, for example, were known to pickle various fruits and vegetables, and their conquests helped spread the technique throughout Europe. In the Middle Ages, pickled foods were a staple in the diets of Europeans, especially during winter months when fresh produce was scarce. Meanwhile, in Asia, techniques for fermenting soybeans evolved into what we now know as soy sauce, miso, and tempeh, showcasing the versatility and innovation in fermentation practices across different cultures.

The scientific understanding of pickling and fermenting processes evolved over time. It was not until the 19th century that Louis Pasteur, a French chemist and a microbiologist, discovered the role of microorganisms in fermentation, providing a scientific basis for these age-old practices. This discovery paved the way for advancements in food science and safety, enhancing the efficiency and reliability of pickling and fermenting methods.

Today, pickling and fermenting are experiencing a renaissance, fueled by a growing interest in traditional foods, sustainable living, and the health benefits of probiotics. Artisanal pickles and fermented foods have become increasingly popular and celebrated for their complex flavors and nutritional benefits. Moreover, these practices are being recognized for their potential to engage to food security by reducing food waste and improving the shelf life of perishable items.

The historical background of pickling and fermenting is a testament to the ingenuity and adaptability of human societies in their quest for sustenance and flavor. These practices have not only survived but thrived, adapting to new cultures and technologies while retaining their essence. They embody a connection to our ancestors, reminding us of the timeless importance of food preservation in human history. As we continue to explore the culinary and nutritional possibilities of pickling and fermenting, we pay homage to a tradition that has nourished and enriched human life for millennia.

## Benefits of Pickling and Fermenting in Prepping

In the realm of preparedness and self-sufficiency, the practices of pickling and fermenting stand out as invaluable techniques for food preservation. These ancient methods, refined over centuries, offer many benefits beyond merely extending the shelf life of food. They enhance nutritional value, improve food safety, and offer economic advantages, making them essential skills for anyone interested in prepping and sustainable living.

Pickling and fermenting are processes that naturally preserve food by creating an acidic environment, either by adding vinegar or through the natural production of lactic acid by beneficial bacteria. This environment inhibits the growth of harmful bacteria, effectively preserving the food. These methods have been harnessed throughout history, providing reliable means to store food for extended periods, especially crucial in times of scarcity or when fresh produce is not available.

One of the most significant benefits of pickling and fermenting in prepping is the nutritional enhancement these methods provide. Fermented foods are recognized for their probiotic qualities, offering a boost to the gut microbiome, which is essential for a healthy digestive system. Foods like sauerkraut, kimchi, and kefir are rich in beneficial bacteria, vitamins, and enzymes that can aid digestion, enhance nutrient absorption, and even boost the immune system. In a prepping scenario, maintaining a balanced diet and ensuring adequate intake of necessary nutrients can be challenging. Incorporating pickled and fermented foods into the diet can help address this challenge, providing vital nutrients and promoting overall health.

Furthermore, fermenting can increase the bioavailability of nutrients, making it easier for the body to absorb them. For example, fermenting soybeans to make tempeh significantly increases the digestibility of the protein and the absorption of minerals like iron and calcium. This aspect of fermentation is particularly beneficial in prepping, where maximizing the nutritional value of stored food is crucial for long-term sustenance.

Another significant benefit is food safety. The acidic environment created by pickling and fermenting is hostile to many pathogens that cause food spoilage and foodborne illnesses. This natural barrier enhances the safety of preserved foods, an essential consideration in prepping, where reliance on preserved food is high, and medical resources may be limited. The ability to safely preserve various foods, including vegetables, fruits, meats, and dairy, through these methods provides a diversified and safe food supply.

Economically, pickling and fermenting are cost-effective methods of food preservation. They require minimal equipment and resources, often just salt, water, and the natural bacteria in the environment or the food itself. This makes them accessible to virtually anyone, regardless of budget constraints. For preppers, the ability to preserve their own food reduces reliance on commercially preserved foods, which can be expensive and less nutritious. Additionally, these methods allow for preserving seasonal produce, which can be sourced cheaply or even grown at home, further reducing food costs and ensuring access to fresh-tasting, nutritious food year-round.

The sustainability aspect of pickling and fermenting also aligns with the ethos of prepping, which often emphasizes self-reliance and minimizing waste. These methods allow for the full utilization of harvests, reducing food waste by preserving excess produce that might otherwise spoil. In a world where food security is an increasing concern, efficiently preserving food contributes to resilience and sustainability.

Moreover, the versatility of pickled and fermented foods adds variety to the prepper's diet, breaking the monotony of stored grains and canned goods. These foods' unique flavors and textures can enhance meals, making them more enjoyable and palatable. This is particularly important in stress-filled scenarios, where morale and mental well-being are as crucial as physical health.

In addition to these practical benefits, pickling and fermenting also offer a psychological advantage. The process of preparing and preserving food can provide a sense of control and preparedness, which is comforting in uncertain times. It connects individuals to traditional skills and knowledge, fostering a sense of community and continuity with past generations.

In conclusion, the benefits of pickling and fermenting in prepping are multifaceted, encompassing nutritional, safety, economic, and psychological aspects. These time-honored practices not only ensure a stable and safe food supply but also enhance the quality and enjoyment of the prepper's diet. By incorporating pickling and fermenting into their skill set, preppers can improve their resilience, health, and well-being, preparing them to face uncertain futures confidently. As we look toward a world where self-sufficiency and sustainability are increasingly valued, pickling and fermenting are essential techniques in the prepper's toolkit, bridging the gap between traditional wisdom and modern preparedness strategies.

# CHAPTER II

# The Science Behind Pickling and Fermenting

## Understanding the Fermentation Process

The fermentation process is a fascinating and complex biochemical phenomenon that humans have utilized for thousands of years, yet it continues to captivate and intrigue scientists and culinary enthusiasts alike. From its most fundamental level, fermentation is a metabolic process that, in the absence of oxygen, turns sugar into acids, gases, or alcohol. This process, carried out by various microorganisms including yeasts and bacteria, not only allows for the preservation of foods but also enhances their nutritional value, flavor profile, and digestibility.

Understanding the fermentation process requires a dive into the microscopic world of these microorganisms. Yeasts, for instance, are responsible for the alcoholic fermentation process, where they consume sugar and convert it into ethanol and carbon dioxide. This principle underlies the production of beer, wine, and other alcoholic beverages. On the other hand, lactic acid bacteria play a crucial role in lacto-fermentation, a process that produces lactic acid from carbohydrates. This type of fermentation is key to creating yogurt, sauerkraut, kimchi, and other fermented dairy and vegetable products.

The fermentation process begins when the microorganisms are introduced to a food source containing carbohydrates, such as sugars and starches.

These microorganisms can be naturally present in the food or environment, or they can be added intentionally in the form of a starter culture. Once introduced, they start metabolizing the carbohydrates in an anaerobic (oxygen-free) environment, producing various byproducts depending on the type of fermentation.

One of the most intriguing aspects of fermentation is the diversity of products it can create. The specific outcomes of fermentation—whether it results in alcohol, lactic acid, acetic acid, or other compounds—depend on the types of microorganisms involved, the substrates they feed on, and the environmental conditions, such as temperature, pH, as well as the presence of oxygen. This variability allows for various fermented foods and beverages, each with unique flavors and textures.

Beyond its culinary applications, the fermentation process offers significant health benefits. Fermented foods are known for their probiotic content, which refers to beneficial bacteria that contribute to gut health. These probiotics can help balance the gut microbiota, improving digestion and bolstering the immune system. Moreover, fermentation can increase the bioavailability of nutrients, making it easier for the body to absorb vitamins and minerals from food. For example, fermentation breaks down phytates, compounds that can inhibit the absorption of iron, zinc, as well as calcium, thereby enhancing the nutritional profile of fermented foods.

The fermentation process also plays a pivotal role in food preservation. By producing alcohol or acid, fermentation creates an environment that is inhospitable to pathogenic bacteria, which can cause food spoilage and illness. This natural preservation method has been a cornerstone of human survival, enabling societies to store food for longer periods, particularly in times before refrigeration and modern food preservation techniques.

The science of fermentation has evolved significantly over the centuries, from ancient practices based on trial and error to a sophisticated field of study in microbiology and biochemistry. Today, researchers continue to explore fermentation mechanisms, seeking to understand how specific strains of microorganisms influence fermented products' flavor, texture, and health properties. This ongoing research has led to innovations in food technology, including developing new fermented foods and optimizing fermentation processes for industrial production.

Despite its ancient origins, fermentation is remarkably relevant in contemporary society. The growing interest in sustainable living and natural food production has led to a resurgence in home fermentation practices. Enthusiasts are rediscovering the joys and benefits of making their own yogurt, sourdough bread, kombucha, and more, embracing the fermentation process as both an art and a science.

Moreover, the fermentation process embodies the concept of sustainability, as it often utilizes parts of ingredients that would otherwise be discarded. For example, the fermentation of vegetable scraps into pickles or kimchi reduces food waste while creating nutritious and flavorful products. This aspect of fermentation underscores its potential to contribute to more sustainable food systems and reduce the environmental impact of food production.

In conclusion, fermentation is a multifaceted biochemical phenomenon that has played a crucial role in human civilization. Its applications in food preservation, enhancement of nutritional value, and creation of diverse and flavorful foods and beverages underscore its importance. The health benefits associated with fermented foods and their role in sustainable food practices highlight the enduring value of fermentation in promoting well-being and environmental stewardship. As we continue to explore and understand the complexities of fermentation, it remains a testament to the ingenuity of human cultures and the wonders of the natural world.

## Role of Microorganisms in Pickling and Fermenting

The role of microorganisms in pickling and fermenting is a fascinating and intricate process that underscores the intersection of biology, chemistry, and culinary arts. These tiny, often invisible, life forms are responsible for transforming raw ingredients into flavorful, preserved foods that have been staples in human diets for thousands of years. Understanding the role of these microorganisms not only sheds light on the science behind pickling and fermenting but also reveals the complexity and diversity of these ancient preservation techniques.

At the heart of pickling and fermenting is preserving food in a way that enhances its flavor, nutritional value, and shelf life. While the methods may vary, the fundamental principle involves creating conditions that favor the growth of beneficial microorganisms while inhibiting harmful ones. This is achieved through the control of environmental factors such as temperature, salinity, and pH levels.

In fermentation, microorganisms such as bacteria, yeasts, and molds play the central role. These organisms metabolize the natural sugars found in foods, converting them into alcohol, carbon dioxide, and organic acids. The lactic acid bacteria (LAB), including species such as Lactobacillus, Leuconostoc, and Pediococcus, are essential in the fermentation of vegetables, dairy products, and meats. These bacteria thrive in anaerobic (oxygen-free) conditions and moderate salt concentrations, producing lactic acid as a byproduct of metabolism. The lactic acid not only preserves the food by lowering the pH but also imparts a tangy flavor that is characteristic of fermented foods. Moreover, the process of lactic acid fermentation enhances the digestibility and nutritional profile of foods, increasing the availability of vitamins and minerals, and introducing beneficial probiotics that support gut health.

In pickling, the preservation and flavoring of food are achieved through immersion in an acidic solution, typically vinegar, or through fermentation that produces acid naturally. In vinegar pickling, the high acidity of the solution prevents microbial growth, preserving the food. However, fermentation-based pickling relies on natural or added microorganisms to produce an acidic environment. Like lactic acid fermentation, this method encourages the growth of LAB, which converts sugars into lactic acid, thereby pickling the food. This not only extends the shelf life of the product but also enriches it with flavors and nutrients.

The role of yeasts in fermentation, particularly in the production of alcoholic beverages as well as bread, is another example of the importance of microorganisms. Yeasts, such as Saccharomyces cerevisiae, metabolize sugars to produce alcohol and carbon dioxide, resulting in the fermentation of beer, wine, and the leavening of bread. While not typically associated with pickling, certain types of fermentation, such as that used to produce kombucha, rely on symbiotic cultures of bacteria and yeast (SCOBY) to ferment sweetened tea into a tangy, effervescent drink rich in probiotics.

The microbial ecosystems involved in pickling and fermenting are intricate and can vary greatly from one culture and environment to another. The specific strains of microorganisms that thrive in a particular fermentation process can be influenced by factors such as the local climate, the ingredients used, and even the equipment and techniques employed. This diversity is part of what gives fermented and pickled foods their unique flavors and characteristics, with specific strains sometimes becoming closely associated with particular regional foods.

Controlling the fermentation and pickling process is crucial to ensure safety and gain the desired outcomes despite the reliance on naturally occurring or deliberately introduced microorganisms. Uncontrolled microbial growth can lead to the proliferation of harmful bacteria, spoiling the food and posing health risks. Therefore, maintaining proper hygiene, temperature, and salinity levels is essential to promote the rise of beneficial microorganisms while inhibiting pathogenic ones.

The role of microorganisms in pickling and fermenting extends beyond mere food preservation. These processes also contribute to the cultural and gastronomic heritage of societies worldwide. Fermented and pickled foods often hold significant cultural value, symbolizing the ingenuity and traditions of the people who create them. From the kimchi of Korea to the sauerkraut of Germany, these foods are a testament to the profound relationship between humans and the microorganisms that support our survival and enrich our diets.

In conclusion, the role of microorganisms in pickling and fermenting is both complex and essential. These microscopic entities are the driving force behind the transformation of simple ingredients into diverse, flavorful, and nutritious foods that have sustained and delighted humans for millennia. Through the careful manipulation of environmental conditions, humans have harnessed the power of these microorganisms, creating a vast array of preserved foods that serve as a testament to our culinary creativity and contribute to our health and well-being. As we continue to explore and understand the microbial world, the possibilities for innovation and discovery in pickling and fermenting remain boundless, promising new flavors, improved nutrition, and deeper connections to our cultural heritage.

## Factors Influencing Fermentation Success

The success of fermentation, a process revered both for its capacity to preserve food and enhance nutritional and organoleptic properties, is influenced by a myriad of factors. This biological process, driven by microorganisms such as bacteria, yeasts, and molds, transforms food substrates into products with extended shelf life and often improved taste, aroma, and digestibility. Understanding the factors that influence fermentation success is crucial for both artisanal producers and enthusiasts aiming to harness the full potential of this ancient technique.

Temperature plays a pivotal part in the fermentation process. Each microorganism involved in fermentation operates optimally within a specific temperature range. For instance, the lactic acid bacteria responsible for sauerkraut and yogurt fermentation thrive at temperatures within 20 degree Celcius and 30 degree Celcius (68°F to 86°F). Deviations from these optimal conditions can slow down the fermentation process or lead to the proliferation of undesirable microorganisms, compromising the safety and quality of the final product. Thus, controlling the temperature is essential for achieving a successful fermentation.

The pH level, or the acidity of the fermentation environment, is another critical factor. Most fermentative microorganisms prefer a slightly acidic environment to begin with, which they then contribute to lowering further as fermentation progresses. This drop in pH naturally inhibits the growth of spoilage organisms and pathogens, ensuring the safety and longevity of the fermented product. For example, the initial acidity in vegetable fermentation helps to select for beneficial lactic acid bacteria over harmful microbes. When necessary, monitoring and adjusting the pH can help steer the fermentation towards success.

Salinity, or salt concentration, is also paramount in fermentation, especially in vegetable and dairy fermentations. Salt acts as a selective pressure, favoring the growth of lactic acid bacteria while inhibiting spoilage organisms and pathogens. The right salt concentration can ensure a safe and successful fermentation by creating an environment conducive to the desired microbial populations. However, too much salt can inhibit fermentation altogether, while too little may not effectively suppress harmful microbes.

The substrate's quality and preparation significantly influence fermentation outcomes. Fresh, high-quality ingredients free from contaminants are more likely to yield successful fermentations. The manner in which these substrates are prepared, including their size, shape, and the consistency of their preparation, can affect how well microorganisms can colonize and ferment the food. For instance, finely shredded cabbage for sauerkraut provides a larger surface area for bacteria to work on, facilitating a quicker and more uniform fermentation.

Oxygen availability is another factor influencing fermentation. While aerobic fermentations require oxygen, anaerobic fermentations, such as those involved in making yogurt, sauerkraut, and many other traditional fermented foods, do not. In anaerobic fermentations, eliminating or reducing oxygen exposure is crucial to hinder the growth of unwanted aerobic microorganisms that could spoil the food. Techniques such as submerging the ferment under brine or using airlock systems are employed to create anaerobic conditions conducive to successful fermentation.

Microbial culture selection is integral to the success of controlled fermentations, where specific strains of microorganisms are introduced to the substrate. The choice of culture affects the final product's fermentation rate, flavor, texture, and safety. Using pure, active cultures with known properties can lead to consistent and high-quality outcomes. In spontaneous fermentations, where the natural microbial flora of the ingredients kickstarts the process, the environment and handling practices play an important role in determining the microbial communities that will dominate the fermentation.

Lastly, the fermentation vessel and environment contribute to the success of the process. Materials that are non-reactive and easy to clean, such as glass, ceramic, or food-grade plastic, are preferred to avoid contamination and chemical reactions that could affect the fermentation. The cleanliness of the fermentation environment, including the tools and containers used, cannot be overstated. Proper sanitation prevents the introduction of spoilage organisms and pathogens that could outcompete the desired microorganisms or produce harmful substances.

In conclusion, the success of fermentation is not attributable to a single factor but rather to a complex interplay of conditions that favor the growth and activity of beneficial microorganisms. Temperature, pH, salinity, substrate quality and preparation, oxygen availability, microbial culture selection, and the fermentation vessel and environment each play critical roles in determining the outcome of the fermentation process. By carefully managing these factors, producers and hobbyists alike can achieve successful fermentations, creating safe, nutritious, and delicious products. This understanding empowers individuals to explore the rich world of fermented foods and connects them to an age-old tradition that has been a cornerstone of human culture and survival.

## Safety Considerations in Pickling and Fermenting

Safety considerations in pickling and fermenting are paramount for ensuring the healthfulness and quality of the end products. While largely safe and effective, these ancient food preservation methods involve biological processes that require careful management to prevent the growth of harmful microorganisms. Understanding and adhering to safety protocols is essential for anyone engaging in these practices, whether at a commercial scale or as a home hobbyist.

The process of pickling typically involves submerging foods in an acidic solution, often vinegar, or through fermentation in which the food creates its own acidic environment, typically through the action of lactic acid bacteria. Conversely, fermentation relies on the controlled activity of various microorganisms, including yeasts and bacteria, to convert sugars and other carbohydrates into alcohol, carbon dioxide, and organic acids. While these processes naturally inhibit the growth of many pathogens, specific safety considerations must be observed to ensure that the finished products are tasty and safe to consume.

One of the primary safety concerns in pickling and fermenting is the prevention of contamination by harmful microorganisms, such as pathogenic bacteria, molds, and yeasts that can spoil food and potentially cause foodborne illnesses. To mitigate this risk, strict hygiene practices must be followed. This includes thoroughly washing hands, using clean utensils and containers, and ensuring the ingredients are fresh and free from visible spoilage. The use of sterilized equipment cannot be overstated, as it prevents the introduction of unwanted microbes that could outcompete the beneficial ones or produce toxins.

Another critical safety consideration is properly managing the fermentation environment, particularly controlling temperature and pH. Most pickling and fermenting processes require specific temperature ranges to encourage the growth of desirable microorganisms while inhibiting harmful ones. For example, vegetable fermentation typically occurs at room temperature, around 18°C to 22°C (64°F to 72°F), which is optimal for the activity of lactic acid bacteria. Deviating from these temperature ranges can lead to the proliferation of unwanted microbes, spoiling the food and making it unsafe.

The acidity of the pickling or fermenting environment is equally crucial. A sufficiently acidic environment, typically a pH of 4.6 or lower, inhibits the growth of most pathogens. Monitoring the pH throughout the fermentation process, therefore, helps ensure safety. In cases where the natural fermentation does not achieve a low enough pH, it may be necessary to add vinegar or another acidulant to adjust the acidity and secure the product's safety.

Salt concentration is also a key factor in the safety of fermented foods. Salt inhibits the growth of undesirable microorganisms while promoting the fermentation process by lactic acid bacteria. However, the correct salt concentration is necessary; too little may not effectively inhibit harmful microbes, while too much can halt the fermentation process entirely.

Ensuring the correct balance of ingredients is another important safety measure. Incorrect ratios of salt, sugar, or acid can lead to incomplete fermentation or preservation, creating opportunities for spoilage and the growth of harmful bacteria, including Clostridium botulinum, the bacterium that causes botulism. Recipes and methods should be followed accurately, especially for those new to pickling and fermenting, to ensure that the conditions are unfavorable for the growth of such pathogens.

Botulism, while rare, is a serious consideration in anaerobic (oxygen-free) environments, such as those created in certain types of fermenting and canning. The toxin produced by Clostridium botulinum is highly dangerous, even in minute quantities. Ensuring that foods are fermented or pickled under conditions that prevent the growth of this bacterium is critical. This includes using the correct type of salt (non-iodized), avoiding the use of metal containers that can react with acids, and following trusted recipes and guidelines.

Monitoring the fermentation process and recognizing signs of spoilage is vital. Signs that a fermentation has gone awry include the presence of mold, an off or unpleasant smell, and a bulging container, indicating the production of excess gas by undesirable microorganisms. If there is any doubt about the safety of a fermented or pickled product, it is better to err on the side of caution and discard it.

In conclusion, while pickling and fermenting are age-old and generally safe methods of food preservation, they require careful attention to safety considerations to ensure that the products are delicious and safe to consume. By adhering to proper hygiene practices, controlling the fermentation environment, accurately balancing ingredients, and being vigilant for signs of spoilage, enthusiasts and professionals alike can enjoy the benefits of these traditional food preservation methods without risking health. Through such diligence, the rich flavors and nutritional benefits of pickled and fermented foods can be safely enjoyed, continuing a culinary tradition that has nourished humans for millennia.

# CHAPTER III

# Basic Pickling Techniques

## Equipment and Ingredients Needed

Pickling, a method of preserving food that has been practiced for thousands of years, involves immersing foods in an acidic solution or through fermentation in brine to extend their shelf life and enhance their flavors. This process, deeply rooted in culinary traditions worldwide, requires specific equipment and ingredients to ensure success and safety. Understanding what is needed for pickling can help beginners and seasoned practitioners alike to prepare delicious pickled foods while adhering to safety standards.

The essential equipment for pickling includes jars, lids, and a large pot for boiling water, commonly known as a water bath canner. Glass jars with tight-sealing lids are preferred because they do not react with the acidic pickling solution, ensuring the flavor and safety of the pickled product. Mason jars, which come in various sizes, are popular due to their wide availability and the reliable sealing capabilities of their two-part lids. The lids are crucial for creating an airtight seal that prevents contamination and spoilage. It's essential to use new lids each time to guarantee a secure seal, although the screw bands that hold the lids in place can be reused.

A water bath canner, essentially a large, deep pot with a rack, is used for processing jars in boiling water. This step is critical for killing any harmful bacteria and ensuring the jars are sealed properly for shelf-stable storage. The rack prevents the jars from shattering and ensures that they are kept off the bottom of the pot, which allows for even heat dispersion of the contents of the pot. Any large, deep pot that has a lid can be utilized as a substitute for a water bath canner for individuals who do not possess one. The only requirement is that the pot must be deep enough to cover the jars with water that is at least one inch deep above them.

Other important tools include a jar lifter, for safely removing hot jars from boiling water; a funnel, to transfer pickles and brine into jars without spillage; and a bubble remover, or a non-metallic spatula, to release any air bubbles trapped in the jar before sealing. A headspace tool, or a ruler, can be used to ensure the proper amount of space is left between the top of the food and the rim of the jar, which is crucial for achieving a good seal.

The ingredients for pickling are equally important and start with the primary food item, such as vegetables, fruits, meats, or eggs. Fresh, high-quality produce free from bruises and blemishes is essential for the best pickling results, owing to the fact that the finished product is affected directly by the quality of the ingredients. The brine, a vinegar and water solution, acts as the pickling medium. With its acetic acid content, vinegar is responsible for the acidic environment that preserves the food. It's important to use vinegar with at least 5% acidity, and many recipes call for white distilled or apple cider vinegar due to their neutral and complementary flavors, respectively.

Salt is another crucial ingredient, serving to flavor the pickles as well as contribute to the preservation process by creating an environment where harmful bacteria struggle to survive. When pickling, it's essential to use pickling or canning salt, which is pure sodium chloride without the anti-caking agents or iodine found in table salt; these additives can discolor the pickles and cloud the brine.

Spices as well as herbs are used to add flavor to pickles, with typical choices including dill, garlic, mustard seed, peppercorns, and bay leaves. The specific combination of spices and herbs can be adjusted depending on personal preference as well as the type of pickle being made. Depending on the recipe, sugar is sometimes added to the brine to balance the acidity and add sweetness to the final product.

Water used in the brine should be free of impurities. Hard water, in particular, can interfere with the pickling process and affect the texture and appearance of the pickles. If the tap water is hard or contains high levels of minerals, using filtered or bottled water is advisable.

In conclusion, successful pickling requires not only a knowledge of the process but also the right equipment and ingredients. Glass jars with new lids, a water bath canner, and tools like a jar lifter, funnel, and bubble remover are essential for safely processing and storing pickled foods. High-quality produce, vinegar with sufficient acidity, pickling salt, and a selection of spices and herbs are the foundational ingredients that contribute to the flavor and preservation of pickled items. With these tools and ingredients, anyone can embark on the rewarding journey of pickling, enjoying the delicious results while paying homage to a time-honored culinary tradition.

## Step-by-Step Guide to Pickling Vegetables

Pickling vegetables is a time-honored tradition combining the art of preservation with fermentation and acidity to create flavorful, long-lasting provisions. This culinary practice, which spans cultures and centuries, not only extends the shelf life of fresh produce but also enhances its taste and nutritional value. A step-by-step guide to pickling vegetables involves preparing the produce, creating the pickling brine, sterilizing the jars, packing the vegetables, processing the jars, and finally storing the finished product. This section delves into each of these steps to provide a comprehensive overview of the pickling process.

The first step in pickling vegetables is the preparation of the produce. Selecting fresh, high-quality vegetables is crucial, as the quality of the ingredients directly impacts the final outcome. The vegetables should be washed thoroughly under cold water to remove any dirt or debris. Depending on the recipe and personal preference, the vegetables can then be sliced, chopped, or left whole. It's essential to ensure that the pieces are uniform in size to guarantee even pickling.

Once the vegetables are prepared, the next step is to create the pickling brine. The brine is a solution of vinegar, water, salt, and often sugar, heated until the salt and sugar dissolve completely. The choice of vinegar can vary—white vinegar is commonly used for its clear color and neutral flavor, while apple cider vinegar adds a fruity note. The salt should be non-iodized, as iodine can cloud the brine and affect the texture of the vegetables. Spices and herbs, such as dill, garlic, mustard seeds, and peppercorns, can be added to the brine for additional flavor. The proportion of vinegar to water and the amount of salt and sugar depending on the recipe and the desired taste and preservation level.

Sterilizing the jars and lids is a critical step to prevent contamination and ensure the safety of the pickled vegetables. The jars can be sterilized by boiling them in water for 10 minutes or washing them in a dishwasher on a hot cycle. The lids should be prepared according to the manufacturer's instructions, typically involving simmering them in hot water rather than boiling to ensure the seal's integrity.

Packing the vegetables into the jars is done with care to maximize space while ensuring that there is enough room for the brine to cover the vegetables completely. A canning funnel can be used to neatly transfer the vegetables into the jars. The prepared brine is then poured over the vegetables, leaving a headspace at the top of the jar as the recipe recommends, usually about a half-inch. This space is necessary to allow for the expansion of the liquid during the processing stage. A bubble remover or a non-metallic spatula can be used to gently tap the jars and release any air bubbles trapped between the vegetables.

Processing the jars to seal them involves placing them in a water bath canner or a large pot with a rack at the bottom. The jars should be covered with water by at least an inch and then brought to a boil. The boiling time varies depending on the recipe and altitude, but it is typically between 10 to 15 minutes. This step is essential for creating a vacuum seal on the jars, which preserves the vegetables and prevents spoilage.

Finally, storing the pickled vegetables correctly is crucial for maintaining their quality and safety. Once the jars have been processed, they should be removed from the water bath and allowed to cool on a towel or rack without touching for 24 hours. The seal should be checked by pressing down on the center of the lid; if it doesn't pop back, the jar is sealed properly. Any jars that haven't sealed can be refrigerated and consumed within a few weeks. Properly sealed jars should be stored in a cool, dark place and can last for up to a year. Before consuming, it's a good practice to check for any signs of spoilage, which includes off odors, colors, or textures.

In summary, pickling vegetables is a rewarding process that allows for preserving the harvest and enjoying flavorful, nutritious foods year-round. By following these steps—preparing the produce, creating the brine, sterilizing the jars, packing the vegetables, processing the jars, and storing the finished product—anyone can successfully pickle vegetables at home. This guide offers a foundation upon which to explore the vast and varied world of pickling, encouraging culinary creativity and a deeper appreciation for this ancient preservation method.

## Recipes for Basic Pickling Solutions

The art of pickling is a culinary tradition that has been passed down through generations, allowing us to preserve a taste of the harvest long after the growing season has ended. At the heart of this preservation method is the pickling solution, a simple yet transformative mixture of vinegar, water, salt, and sometimes sugar, infused with various spices and herbs to create flavors that range from sharply tangy to sweetly spiced. This section explores recipes for basic pickling solutions, each designed to cater to different tastes as well as preferences, providing a foundation upon which both novices and seasoned picklers can build.

The Classic Dill Pickle Brine is perhaps the most iconic of all pickling solutions, celebrated for its crisp tartness and aromatic dill flavor. A big saucepan should be used to combine four cups of water, two cups of white vinegar, and two teaspoons of non-iodized pickling salt in order to complete the preparation of this brine. While the mixture is being brought to a boil, make sure that the salt is completely dissolved. Adding garlic cloves, mustard seeds, and fresh dill to the jars before adding the cucumbers introduces the brine's flavor depth. This solution is perfect for cucumbers but can also be used with green beans, carrots, and even asparagus, offering a versatile base for experimenting with different vegetables.

For those with a penchant for sweetness in their pickles, the Bread and Butter Pickle Brine offers a delightful balance of sweet as well as tangy. Start with 3 cups of white vinegar and 3 cups of sugar, adding 1/4 cup of pickling salt to a pot. Heat gently, stirring until the sugar and the salt dissolve completely. The inclusion of turmeric, celery seed, and mustard seed gives this brine its distinctive flavor, reminiscent of old-fashioned bread and butter pickles. This brine pairs wonderfully with thinly sliced cucumbers, onions, and even peppers, creating a condiment that shines alongside sandwiches and burgers.

For enthusiasts of fiery flavors, the Spicy Pickle Brine introduces heat to the pickling process. This brine combines 3 cups of water, 3 cups of apple cider vinegar, as well as 2 tablespoons of pickling salt. To infuse the brine with heat, add sliced jalapeños, crushed red pepper flakes, and a few cloves of garlic to the jars before packing them with cucumbers or other vegetables. The spicy brine is an excellent choice for those looking to add a kick to their pickles, suitable for jazzing up tacos and nachos or simply enjoying as a bold snack.

The Asian-Inspired Pickle Brine takes inspiration from the flavors of the East, incorporating soy sauce and rice vinegar for a distinctively umami-rich profile. Combine 2 cups of rice vinegar, 1 cup of water, one-half cup of soy sauce, and also 1/4 cup of sugar in a saucepan, heating until the sugar dissolves. Adding slices of ginger, star anise, and a dash of sesame seeds to the jars introduces a complexity that complements the brine's base. This brine works exceptionally well with radishes, carrots, and cucumbers, creating pickles that can elevate rice dishes, salads, and platters with their nuanced flavors.

Finally, the Aromatic Sweet Vinegar Brine offers a European flair, marrying the sweetness of sugar with the depth of aromatic spices. To create this brine, mix 3 cups of apple cider vinegar with 1 cup of sugar, 1 cup of water, and also 2 tablespoons of pickling salt. Adding cinnamon sticks, cloves, and allspice berries to the jars before adding the fruit or vegetables lends a warm, spiced note that is particularly suited to pickling fruits like pears, peaches, and cherries. This brine transforms the produce into a luxurious condiment or dessert topping, showcasing the versatility of pickling beyond vegetables.

In crafting these basic pickling solutions, it's important to remember the flexibility and room for creativity that pickling affords. While the proportions of vinegar, water, salt, and sugar form the backbone of the brine, adding spices and herbs is where the magic truly happens, allowing each batch of pickles to tell its unique flavor story. Whether adhering to these recipes or embarking on a journey of customization, the key to successful pickling lies in the balance of flavors, the quality of the ingredients, and the joy of creation.

Using these recipes for basic pickling solutions, we are able to investigate the diverse array of flavors that can be achieved through the process of pickling. From the crisp tang of a classic dill pickle to the sweet warmth of spiced fruits, pickling opens up a world of culinary possibilities. It serves not only as a means of preservation but also as a celebration of flavor, tradition, and the endless creativity that cooking invites. As we delve into the practice of pickling, we connect with generations past and present, continuing the timeless tradition of transforming simple ingredients into something extraordinary.


## Tips for Achieving Flavorful Pickles

Creating flavorful pickles that stand out for their taste and texture is an art that combines tradition with personal touch. Pickling, a method steeped in history, preserves and enhances the flavor of vegetables and fruits through fermentation or vinegar brining. Achieving the perfect balance of tanginess, sweetness, and spice requires attention to detail, from selecting the right ingredients to mastering the pickling process. This section explores comprehensive tips for crafting pickles that are a delight to the palate and a testament to the art of pickling.

The foundation of flavorful pickles lies in the quality of the produce used. Freshness is key, as the condition of the vegetables or fruits directly influences the taste and texture of the final product. Choosing firm, ripe, and unblemished produce is essential, as fresh ingredients absorb the brining solution more effectively and retain a crisp texture. Seasonal vegetables and fruits picked at their peak offer the best flavors and nutritional benefits, ensuring the pickles are vibrant and full of character.

Water quality is another critical factor in pickling. Hard water, which have high levels of minerals like calcium and magnesium, can affect the pickles' firmness and the brine's clarity. Using filtered or distilled water ensures that the pickles remain crisp and the brine stays clear, allowing the flavors of the spices and vinegar to shine through without interference.

The choice of vinegar is central to the flavor profile of pickles. White vinegar offers a clean, sharp tang, while apple cider vinegar provides a milder, fruity acidity that complements the natural flavors of the produce. Experimenting with different types of vinegar, such as rice vinegar for a subtle sweetness or red wine vinegar for depth, can add complexity to the pickles. The acidity level of the vinegar, typically around 5%, is crucial for preserving the pickles safely and should not be compromised.

Salt plays a dual role in pickling, acting as a preservative and flavor enhancer. Using non-iodized salt, such as pickling or kosher salt, is essential because iodine can cloud the brine and alter the taste of the pickles. The amount of salt should be balanced to ensure the pickles are neither too salty nor bland, enhancing the natural flavors of the produce and the aromatic spices.

Spices and herbs are the soul of pickling, infusing the brine with distinctive flavors. Classics such as dill, garlic, mustard seeds, and peppercorns are staples in many pickle recipes, offering a traditional taste. However, exploring a variety of spices and herbs can elevate the pickles to a new level of flavor. Coriander seeds, bay leaves, cinnamon sticks, and cloves can introduce warm, spicy notes, while fresh herbs like tarragon, thyme, and basil add brightness and complexity. Toasting spices before adding them to the brine can intensify their flavors, creating a deeper, more robust taste profile.

The proportion of vinegar, water, and spices in the pickling brine is crucial for achieving the desired flavor balance. A standard ratio is a good starting point, but adjusting the acidity, sweetness, and spice levels according to personal preference allows for customization. Adding a touch of sugar can soften the acidity and also bring out the natural sweetness of the produce, creating a harmonious flavor profile. Similarly, a pinch of chili flakes or sliced hot peppers can introduce a spicy kick for those who enjoy a bit of heat.

Time is an essential ingredient in pickling, as it permits the flavors to meld and develop. While some pickles are ready to eat within a few hours or days, others benefit from weeks or even months of aging. Tasting the pickles periodically can help determine the optimal aging time, ensuring the flavors are fully developed without becoming overly sour or losing their crisp texture.

Finally, experimentation and patience are key to mastering the art of pickling. Each batch of pickles is an opportunity to refine techniques, adjust flavors, and discover new combinations. Keeping detailed notes on the ingredients, proportions, and process can help replicate successful batches and tweak those that didn't quite hit the mark.

In conclusion, achieving flavorful pickles is a blend of science and art, needing attention to detail and a willingness to experiment. By selecting fresh produce, using quality ingredients, and carefully balancing the flavors, it's possible to create pickles that are a testament to the rich tradition of pickling. Whether enjoyed as a tangy snack, a flavorful addition to meals, or a homemade gift, pickles crafted with care and creativity are a culinary delight that celebrates the simple yet profound pleasure of preserving the bounty of the harvest.

# CHAPTER IV

# Advanced Pickling Methods

## Experimenting with Different Vinegars and Spices

Experimenting with different vinegars and spices is a culinary adventure that can transform ordinary dishes into extraordinary experiences. This exploration is not just about altering flavors; it's about understanding how the subtle or dramatic nuances of vinegar and the complexity of spices can influence the overall character of a meal. As we delve into the world of culinary experimentation, we discover that vinegar and spices are not merely ingredients but tools of artistry, capable of elevating the sensory dimensions of food.

Vinegar, with its acidic profile, can brighten and sharpen a dish's flavors. The variety of vinegars available today is a testament to its versatility in the kitchen. From Modena's robust and rich balsamic vinegar to the delicate and sweet rice vinegar used in Asian cuisines, each type offers a unique flavor profile that can enhance different dishes. For example, experimenting with apple cider vinegar can add a fruity tang to salads and marinades, complementing both the sweetness of fruits and the earthiness of greens. With its subtle acidity, white wine vinegar can be used to deglaze pans, adding depth to sauces and gravies. Meanwhile, the dark, syrupy balsamic vinegar can be reduced to a glaze and drizzled over roasted vegetables or strawberries, adding a complex sweetness and acidity that heightens the natural flavors of the food.

Exploring spices opens up a world where colors, aromas, and flavors intermingle to create a tapestry of taste. Spices, the dried seeds, fruits, roots, or bark of plants, have been used for millennia to season and preserve food. Each spice carries its own history and cultural significance, from the peppercorns that were once worth their weight in gold to the cinnamon that fueled ancient trade routes. Experimenting with spices means more than just adding heat or sweetness to a dish; it's about layering flavors to build depth and complexity.

For instance, the warmth of cinnamon can be paired with the sweetness of sugar in baked goods or used in savory dishes, such as Moroccan tagines, to add a subtle richness. The fiery heat of chili powder can be moderated with the smokiness of paprika or the citrusy zing of lime zest, creating a balanced spice blend perfect for grilling meats or seasoning vegetables. The earthy tones of cumin, often used in Middle Eastern and Mexican cuisines, can be combined with the bright freshness of coriander to bring a dish to life, offering a burst of flavor with every bite.

The magic of experimenting with vinegars and spices lies in the balance and harmony achieved through trial and error. Understanding the properties of each vinegar and spice—its acidity, sweetness, heat, and aroma—is crucial in determining how it will interact with other ingredients. For example, a dish with a base of sweet vegetables like carrots or sweet potatoes can be elevated with the addition of apple cider vinegar and a hint of nutmeg, balancing the sweetness with acidity and warmth. Conversely, a rich, fatty dish might benefit from the sharpness of red wine vinegar and the complexity of a spice blend featuring black pepper, thyme, and rosemary, cutting through the richness and adding aromatic depth.

Moreover, experimenting with vinegars and spices is not confined to the realms of traditional cuisines or established recipes. The modern culinary landscape encourages innovation, inviting chefs and home cooks alike to blend the boundaries between cultures and flavors. A classic Italian vinaigrette might be reimagined with rice vinegar and a dash of wasabi powder, marrying Italian and Japanese flavors in a harmonious dressing. Similarly, the traditional spices of a Mexican mole sauce can be infused with a splash of sherry vinegar, introducing a Spanish element that adds brightness and lifts the complex flavors of the sauce.

In embracing the experimental approach to vinegars and spices, one also learns to appreciate flavor nuances and the impact of acidity, heat, and aroma on the sensory experience of eating. It encourages a mindful approach to cooking, where each ingredient is selected and used with intention, contributing to the overall harmony of the dish. This journey of exploration and discovery not only enriches one's culinary repertoire but also deepens the connection to the cultural stories and traditions that spices and vinegars carry with them.

In conclusion, experimenting with different vinegars and spices is essential for anyone looking to elevate their culinary skills and expand their flavor horizons. In order to accomplish this, one must be willing to explore, experiment, and gain knowledge from both successes and failures. Through this process, cooks can unlock the full potential of their ingredients, creating dishes that are not only flavorful but also reflective of their creativity and curiosity. As we continue to explore the vast and varied world of vinegars and spices, we open ourselves up to new tastes, textures, and culinary possibilities, making each meal an adventure waiting to be savored.


## Pickling Fruits and Eggs

Pickling, a method of preservation that has stood the test of time, is not limited to vegetables but extends its flavorful embrace to fruits and eggs, offering a delightful twist to traditional pickled items. This section explores the nuanced art and science behind pickling fruits and eggs, delving into the methods, benefits, and culinary versatility that these pickled delicacies bring to the table.

The process of pickling fruits involves submerging them in a mixture of vinegar, water, sugar, and spices, which not only preserves them but also imparts a unique combination of sweet, tart, and spicy flavors. Fruits like cherries, peaches, pears, and even watermelon rinds can be transformed through pickling, turning them into gourmet treats that elevate the taste of desserts, salads, and cheese platters. The key to successful fruit pickling lies in choosing the right fruits—those that are just ripe, firm, and free of bruises will hold up best in the pickling brine.

The choice of vinegar is crucial in fruit pickling, as its acidity level needs to balance the natural sweetness of the fruits. Lighter vinegars, such as apple cider or white wine vinegar, are often preferred for their subtle flavors that do not overpower the fruits. Adding spices and herbs—such as cinnamon, cloves, vanilla, and star anise— can complement the fruits' flavors, adding depth and complexity to the pickled product. Sugar, meanwhile, is adjusted according to the fruits' natural sweetness and the desired end result, whether it be a more pronounced sweetness or a balanced sweet-tart profile.

On the other hand, pickling eggs is a practice that dates back centuries, offering a savory snack or addition to salads and appetizers. The process begins with hard-boiled eggs that are peeled and then submerged in a vinegar-based brine. The brine, typically more savory and acidic than its fruit pickling counterpart, often includes ingredients like beet juice for color, onions, garlic, and various spices such as dill, mustard seeds, and peppercorns. The acidic environment flavors the eggs and acts as a preservative, allowing them to be stored for several weeks.

The texture of pickled eggs is something to behold; the firmness of the egg whites contrasts with the creaminess of the yolks, creating a delightful mouthfeel. The brine penetrates the eggs, infusing them with its flavors and slightly firming up their texture. The addition of beet juice or turmeric can impart a vibrant color to the eggs, making them as visually appealing as they are tasty.

Both fruit and egg pickling require attention to the brine's acidity level, ensuring it is high enough to preserve the food safely while balancing flavors. The process also demands cleanliness and sterilization of jars and utensils to prevent contamination and spoilage. The jars must be sealed properly and stored in a cool, dark place to enhance the pickling process and ensure the longevity of the pickled products.

The culinary applications of pickled fruits and eggs are vast and varied. Pickled fruits can be used as a condiment for meats, a zesty addition to cocktails, or as a unique topping for ice creams and pastries. They bring a bright burst of flavor that can cut through the richness of dishes, adding a layer of complexity that enhances the dining experience. With their tangy taste and firm texture, pickled eggs make for a protein-rich snack or an intriguing addition to charcuterie boards and salads. They can also be chopped and added to potato or tuna salads for an unexpected twist.

Beyond their culinary uses, pickling fruits and eggs offers nutritional benefits. The vinegar in the brine can aid digestion, while the spices used in the pickling process can have antioxidant properties. However, it is essential to consume pickled foods in moderation due to their high sodium and sugar content.

In conclusion, pickling fruits and eggs is a culinary adventure that extends the boundaries of traditional pickling, inviting both novice and experienced cooks to navigate the depths of flavor that can be achieved. This practice not only preserves the seasons' bounty but also transforms simple ingredients into gourmet delights that can improve a wide array of dishes. Whether serving as a sweet accent to desserts or a savory snack, pickled fruits and eggs embody the creativity and innovation that lie at the heart of culinary arts, offering a testament to the enduring appeal and versatility of pickling.

## Pickling Meats and Fish

Pickling, a preservation technique as ancient as it is versatile, extends its reach beyond the realm of vegetables and fruits to include meats and fish, introducing a spectrum of flavors and textures unique to these protein-rich foods. This section delves into the traditional and innovative methods of pickling meats and fish, exploring the culinary practices that have allowed these foods to be savored beyond their typical shelf life, enhancing their taste and nutritional value.

Pickling meats and fish is grounded in the need to preserve these perishable foods in the days before refrigeration. Historically, pickling was a necessity, allowing communities to store food for the winter months or long voyages. Today, it serves both a practical role in preservation and a culinary role in flavor enhancement. The method involves submerging the meats or fish in a brine or vinegar solution, often with a blend of spices, to create an environment where bacteria necessary for spoilage cannot thrive.

The brine solution, typically a mixture of water, salt, and vinegar, acts as the preservative medium. Salt plays a crucial part in this process, drawing moisture out of the meat through osmosis, which helps to inhibit the growth of spoilage-causing microorganisms. With its acetic acid, vinegar further ensures preservation by creating an acidic environment unfriendly to bacteria. The spices and seasonings added to the brine not only contribute to the preservation process but also infuse the meats and fish with robust flavors. Commonly used spices include peppercorns, bay leaves, cloves, and allspice, each adding its signature to the final product.

Pickling meats requires a careful balance of ingredients and timing. Meats such as pork, beef, and poultry can be pickled, offering a tender texture and complex flavor profile that distinguishes them from their freshly cooked counterparts. The process often involves curing the meat in the brine for several days or even weeks, depending on the recipe and desired outcome. This slow infusion not only preserves the meat but also tenderizes it, resulting in a product that is both flavorful and succulent.

Fish pickling, while sharing similarities with meat pickling, often requires a shorter curing time due to the fish's delicate texture. Popular in many cultures, pickled fish such as herring, mackerel, and salmon are celebrated for their tangy taste and firm texture. For example, in Scandinavian and Eastern European cuisines, pickled herring plays a central role in traditional dishes, prized for its balance of sweet and sour flavors achieved through the pickling process. The method for fish often includes an initial curing stage with salt before the fish is submerged in the vinegar solution, ensuring both preservation and flavor development.

Safety is paramount when pickling meats and fish due to the potential for spoilage as well as foodborne illnesses. The acidity of the pickling solution must be maintained at a level that prevents the growth of harmful bacteria, including botulism. It is crucial to follow recipes from reputable sources and adhere to recommended preservation practices, including the use of proper canning techniques and sterilized equipment. Additionally, storing the pickled meats and fish in a cool, dark place or refrigerating them can help maintain their safety and extend their shelf life.

The culinary applications of pickled meats and fish are diverse and exciting. They can be enjoyed as stand-alone delicacies, incorporated into salads and sandwiches, or used as flavorful additions to main dishes. Pickled meats have the ability to improve the flavor profiles of stews and casseroles, while pickled fish can be an essential component of appetizers and salads. Pickled fish provides a burst of acidity that compliments the intense flavor of other ingredients.

In contemporary cooking, both professional chefs and home cooks are experimenting with pickling meats and fish in order to create novel meals that pay tribute to traditional flavors while also embracing contemporary tastes. This exploration includes using different types of vinegar, such as balsamic or rice vinegar, to achieve unique flavor profiles and experimenting with various spices and herbs to customize the pickling brine.

In conclusion, pickling meats and fish is a practice rich in history and culinary tradition, offering a method to preserve these foods while significantly enhancing their flavors and textures. A wide variety of meats and fish can be transformed into delicacies that are savored for their complex taste profiles through the careful balance of brine, vinegar, and spices. As culinary traditions evolve, the art of pickling meats and fish continues to adapt, inviting both professional chefs and home cooks to explore the depths of flavor achievable through this timeless preservation technique. Whether rooted in necessity or driven by the desire for culinary innovation, pickling meats and fish remains a testament to the ingenuity and versatility of cooks throughout the ages.

## Creative Applications of Pickled Foods

With their vibrant tang and crunch, pickled foods have transcended their traditional roles to become staples in the pantheon of culinary creativity. From the humble beginnings of preserving perishables, pickling has evolved into an art form, offering chefs and home cooks alike the opportunity to infuse dishes with unique flavors and textures. This section explores the myriad of creative applications of pickled foods, demonstrating how they can elevate simple dishes into gastronomic delights.

The essence of pickling lies in its ability to transform the ordinary into the extraordinary. By immersing fruits, vegetables, meats, and even eggs in a brine or vinegar solution, these foods are imbued with a distinctive sourness and a complexity of flavor that can enhance a wide range of dishes. Beyond mere preservation, the creative use of pickled foods in modern cuisine reflects a growing appreciation for the interplay of flavors and the artistry involved in meal preparation.

One of the most innovative applications of pickled foods is in the realm of appetizers and snacks. Pickled vegetables, with their crisp texture and sharp taste, can be utilized to add depth to charcuterie boards and antipasto platters, complementing the richness of cheeses and cured meats. Similarly, pickled fruits can serve as a counterpoint to savory dips and spreads, offering a sweet and tangy contrast that stimulates the palate. Chefs also experiment with pickling unexpected items like watermelon rinds and grapes, introducing diners to new taste sensations.

In salads, pickled foods can play a pivotal role, acting as both a flavor enhancer and a source of acidity that can balance the fattiness of dressings. The inclusion of pickled beets, onions, or radishes can modify a simple green salad into a dish bursting with layers of flavor. Moreover, pickled fruits such as cherries or peaches can add an unexpected sweetness and acidity to grain or leafy salads, creating a delightful interplay of textures and tastes.

Main courses also benefit from the inclusion of pickled elements. Pickled vegetables can be incorporated into sandwiches and burgers as a crunchy, acidic component that cuts through the meat's richness. In Asian cuisines, pickled radishes and cucumbers are essential accompaniments to rich dishes, providing a refreshing contrast. Additionally, pickled fruits can be used as a garnish or component in savory dishes, offering a burst of flavor that complements proteins like pork, chicken, and fish.

The versatility of pickled foods extends to the world of sauces and condiments. Pureed or finely chopped pickled vegetables can be mixed into mayonnaises, aiolis, and salsas, adding a tangy twist to these classic accompaniments. This technique enhances the flavor profiles of the sauces and introduces an element of surprise to dishes that may otherwise seem familiar.

Furthermore, pickled foods have found their way into the world of cocktails and beverages, where their acidity and flavor complexity can add depth to drinks. Pickled cherries or berries can be used in place of traditional garnishes in cocktails, providing a nuanced taste that complements the spirits. Similarly, the brine from pickled vegetables, known as pickle juice, has become a popular ingredient in cocktails, offering a salty, tangy kick that balances the sweetness of mixers.

Desserts, too, can benefit from the creative use of pickled foods. Pickled fruits, with their combination of sweetness and acidity, can be incorporated into cakes, tarts, and ice creams, offering a refreshing contrast to the richness of these dishes. Chefs are exploring the potential of pickled ingredients in creating innovative desserts that challenge traditional flavor boundaries, such as pickled strawberry shortcake or pickled apple pie.

The creative applications of pickled foods are not limited by cuisine or course; they are bounded only by the cook's imagination. The key to successfully incorporating pickled elements into dishes lies in understanding the balance of flavors and how the acidity and tang of pickled foods can complement or contrast with other ingredients. By experimenting with different types of pickles and using them unexpectedly, chefs and home cooks can unlock new dimensions of flavor as well as texture in their dishes.

In conclusion, the creative applications of pickled foods in modern cuisine demonstrate this ancient preservation method's enduring appeal and versatility. Whether used as a garnish, a key ingredient, or a source of inspiration, pickled foods can transform the ordinary into the extraordinary, adding depth, complexity, and intrigue to dishes across all courses. As culinary traditions continue to evolve, the role of pickled foods in enhancing and innovating dishes is sure to expand, reflecting a global appreciation for the art of pickling and its endless possibilities.

# CHAPTER V

# Introduction to Fermentation

## Benefits of Fermented Foods for Gut Health

The significance of gut health in general wellness has garnered significant attention in recent years, with a growing body of research underscoring the vital role of the gut microbiome in digestion, immunity, and even mental health. Amidst this burgeoning interest, fermented foods have emerged as powerful allies in the quest for a healthy gut. These foods, which undergo a natural process of lacto-fermentation where in the natural bacteria feed on the sugar and starch in the food building lactic acid, are not only a tradition spanning cultures worldwide but also a cornerstone in nutritional strategies aimed at enhancing gut health. This section explores the multifaceted benefits of fermented foods for gut health, delving into their nutritional composition, impact on the gut microbiome, and broader health implications.

Fermented foods, ranging from yogurt and kefir to sauerkraut, kimchi, and kombucha, are celebrated for their probiotic content. Probiotics are live microorganisms that, when given to the host in sufficient quantities, cause the host to experience a positive impact on their health. The process of fermentation naturally enriches foods with probiotics, primarily strains of Lactobacilli and Bifidobacteria, which are among the most beneficial for gut health. These probiotics play a crucial role in populating the gut with beneficial bacteria, which are essential for keeping the integrity of the intestinal barrier, aiding in digestion, and combating the growth of harmful bacteria.

The consumption of fermented foods contributes to the diversity of the gut microbiome. A diverse microbiome is a hallmark of good gut health, associated with improved digestion, enhanced immune function, and a reduced risk of diseases, including type 2 diabetes, obesity, as well as inflammatory bowel diseases. Fermented foods introduce a variety of beneficial bacteria to the gut, which can help to balance the microbiome and promote its diversity. This, in turn, supports the body's ability to process and absorb nutrients effectively and to protect against pathogens.

Moreover, fermented foods are often rich in prebiotics, non-digestible food components that selectively stimulate the development or the activity of beneficial microorganisms in the gut. Prebiotics, found in foods such as garlic, onions, and asparagus, act as food for probiotics, fostering a symbiotic relationship that enhances gut health. The combination of prebiotics and probiotics, which is known as synbiotics, can be particularly effective in promoting a healthy gut microbiome.

Fermented foods offer enhanced nutritional benefits beyond their probiotic and prebiotic content. The fermentation process can intensify the bioavailability of nutrients, making them more accessible for absorption by the body. For instance, fermentation can break down compounds that inhibit nutrient absorption, such as phytates in grains and legumes, thereby increasing the levels of bioavailable minerals like iron, zinc, and magnesium. Additionally, some fermented foods are sources of essential nutrients, including B vitamins, vitamin K2, and certain amino acids, which are produced or increased through fermentation.

In addition to positively impacting gut health, fermented foods also have a positive impact on the immune system.

Because the majority of the immune system of the body is located in the gut, the health of the gut is synonymous with the health of the immune system. Additionally, the beneficial bacteria that are present in fermented foods have the capacity to improve the mucosal immune response of the gut, which in turn helps to modify the immune system of the body and protects against pathogens. Furthermore, the anti-inflammatory qualities of particular probiotics have the potential to assist in mitigating the impact of disorders such as irritable bowel syndrome, also known as IBS, and other inflammatory gut diseases.

The gut-brain axis is a term that is commonly used to describe the relationship that exists between psychological well-being and the health of the digestive tract. A number of different pathways, including the production of neurotransmitters like serotonin, which is primarily produced in the gut, are among the ways in which the microbiome of the gut can have an effect on the health and behavior of the brain. The consumption of fermented foods, by promoting a healthy gut microbiome, may positively impact mental well-being, potentially alleviating symptoms of depression and anxiety.

In conclusion, the benefits of fermented foods for gut health are manifold, encompassing the enhancement of the gut microbiome's diversity, the provision of vital nutrients, the strengthening of the immune system, and the potential to positively influence mental health. As natural sources of probiotics and prebiotics, fermented foods represent a simple yet powerful dietary intervention for promoting gut health and, by extension, overall well-being. Incorporating various fermented foods into the diet can be a delicious and also nutritious way to support the complex ecosystem within the gut, underscoring the timeless wisdom inherent in traditional dietary practices while aligning with contemporary nutritional science.

## Equipment and Ingredients for Fermentation

Fermentation is a time-honored culinary practice that harnesses the power of microorganisms to transform ingredients into flavorful, nutritious foods with extended shelf life. This biological process, which has been part of human culture for thousands of years, requires specific equipment and ingredients to facilitate the growth of beneficial bacteria, yeasts, or molds. Understanding the essentials for successful fermentation can unlock a world of culinary possibilities, from tangy sauerkraut and rich yogurt to effervescent kombucha and hearty sourdough bread. This section delves into the key equipment and ingredients necessary for fermentation, highlighting how these components work together to create a hospitable environment for beneficial microbes to thrive.

The cornerstone of any fermentation setup is the vessel in which the fermentation process takes place. Glass jars, ceramic crocks, and food-grade plastic containers are popular choices, each offering unique benefits. Glass jars are widely favored for their non-reactive nature, transparency, which permits for easy monitoring of the fermentation process, and availability in various sizes. Ceramic crocks, traditional in many cultures, are ideal for large-scale fermentations like sauerkraut or kimchi. Their thick walls help maintain a stable temperature, which is crucial for consistent fermentation. While less traditional, food-grade plastic containers provide a lightweight and break-resistant option, though it's essential to ensure they are free from harmful chemicals like BPA.

Lids and airlocks are vital components in controlling the fermentation environment. A tight-fitting lid helps to create an anaerobic (oxygen-free) environment necessary for many types of fermentation. However, the buildup of carbon dioxide, a byproduct of fermentation, requires careful management to avoid excessive pressure. Airlocks, devices that allow gas to escape while preventing outside air from entering, can be invaluable, especially for liquid fermentations like wine, beer, or kombucha. For simpler fermentations, like sauerkraut, a clean cloth or coffee filter that is secured with a rubber band can suffice, allowing gases to escape while keeping contaminants out.

Weights or followers are used to keep fermenting foods submerged below the surface of the liquid, minimizing exposure to air and preventing mold growth or unwanted bacteria. In the case of vegetable fermentations, glass or ceramic weights are commonly used. Alternatively, a smaller jar filled with water can serve as an effective weight when placed inside a larger fermentation jar.

The ingredients for fermentation are just as critical as the equipment. The primary ingredient in any fermentation is the food item to be fermented, whether it's cabbage for sauerkraut, milk for yogurt, tea for kombucha, or flour for sourdough bread. The quality of these base ingredients plays a significant role in the flavor and nutritional value of the final product, with fresh, organic, and locally sourced options often yielding the best results.

Salt is an essential ingredient in many fermentation processes, acting as a selective agent that favors the development of beneficial bacteria while inhibiting harmful ones. Using non-iodized salt, which include sea salt or kosher salt, is essential, as iodine can inhibit microbial growth. The salt concentration varies depending on the recipe and desired outcome, from a light brine for lacto-fermented vegetables to heavily salted environments for certain types of cheese or cured meats.

Starter cultures or inoculants introduce specific strains of bacteria, yeasts, or molds to the fermentation, ensuring a predictable and controlled process. These can be commercially purchased or sourced from a previous batch of fermentation. Examples include yogurt cultures, sourdough starters, and kombucha SCOBYs (symbiotic cultures of bacteria and yeast). While many fermentations can occur spontaneously due to naturally present microorganisms, starter cultures can offer consistency and safety, especially for beginners.

When used in fermentations like brining or creating a starter culture, water should be free of chlorine and other chemicals that can inhibit microbial activity. Filtered, spring, or distilled water is often recommended to ensure the health and activity of the fermenting microorganisms.

Spices and flavorings, though not essential for the fermentation process itself, can add depth and complexity to fermented foods. The choice of spices and herbs is vast, ranging from dill and garlic for pickles to cinnamon and vanilla for fermented beverages. Incorporating these flavorings allows for endless creativity in fermentation, enabling the creation of unique and personalized food products.

In conclusion, the successful fermentation of foods requires understanding the equipment and ingredients involved in the process. The right combination of fermentation vessels, lids, airlocks, weights, base ingredients, salt, starter cultures, water, and spices can create an environment conducive to the growth of beneficial microbes. This, in turn, leads to the production of fermented foods that are not only rich in flavor and nutrition but also imbued with the unique satisfaction that comes from engaging in one of humanity's oldest culinary practices. Whether for health, flavor, or the joy of culinary exploration, the art of fermentation offers a rewarding journey into the world of beneficial microbes.

## Fermentation Vessels and Storage Options

Fermentation, a process as ancient as civilization itself, has been a cornerstone of culinary and preservation techniques around the globe. Central to this transformative practice is the choice of fermentation vessels and storage options, which play crucial roles in successfully converting raw ingredients into complex, flavorful, and nutritious fermented products. This section explores the various vessels used for fermentation, their unique characteristics, and the considerations for storing fermented goods to maintain their quality and extend shelf life.

Fermentation vessels are selected based on the fermentation type, the produce quantity, and the fermenting microorganisms' specific requirements. Traditional and modern kitchens employ a range of containers, from simple glass jars to sophisticated stainless steel tanks, each offering distinct advantages for fermentation.

Glass jars are among the most popular choices for home fermentation due to their wide availability, affordability, and inert nature, which ensures that no unwanted flavors are imparted to the ferment. Glass allows for the visual monitoring of the fermentation process, enabling enthusiasts to observe the development of bubbles, changes in color, and the formation of sediment, which are all indicators of fermentation activity. However, glass is fragile and can be heavy, especially in larger sizes, which may limit its use for larger batches.

Ceramic crocks have been used for centuries in various cultures for fermenting vegetables, such as sauerkraut and kimchi. These vessels often come with weights that fit snugly inside to keep the ferment submerged under its brine, creating an anaerobic environment essential for lacto-fermentation. The porous nature of ceramic can be beneficial, allowing for slight air exchange, which can be advantageous for certain ferments. However, to prevent contamination, it's crucial to ensure that ceramic crocks are lead-free and glazed with food-safe materials.

Plastic containers, specifically those made from food-grade plastic, offer a lightweight and unbreakable alternative to glass and ceramic. They are suitable for various fermentation projects, including vegetables, kefir, and yogurt. Despite their convenience, ongoing debate exists about plastic's potential to leach chemicals into food, especially under acidic conditions. Therefore, it is recommended to use plastics labeled as food-safe and free from BPA and other harmful compounds.

Stainless steel vessels are favored for their durability and ease of cleaning, making them an excellent option for large-scale fermentations. Stainless steel is non-reactive, ensuring that no undesirable flavors are transferred to the ferment. This material is prevalent in commercial fermentation setups, such as breweries and wineries, where hygiene and the ability to withstand frequent cleaning are paramount. However, the initial investment for high-quality stainless steel containers can be significant.

Wooden barrels have a long history in the fermentation of beverages, especially wine and beer. Wood, mainly oak, can impart desirable flavors and tannins to the ferment, adding complexity to the finished product. However, wooden vessels require meticulous maintenance to prevent contamination and are more commonly used in commercial operations than in home fermentation.

Once the fermentation process is complete, proper storage is necessary to preserve the quality and extend the shelf life of fermented products. The ideal storage conditions depend on the specific ferment, but most fermented foods benefit from cool, dark environments that slow down fermentation activity and prevent spoilage.

Refrigeration is the most common method for storing fermented foods, significantly slowing microbial activity and preserving the ferment's texture, flavor, and nutritional value. Fermented vegetables, dairy products like yogurt and kefir, and condiments such as pickles and sauces can be stored in the refrigerator for several months.

Cellaring, or storing in a cool basement or cellar, is a traditional method that predates refrigeration. This approach is suitable for large batches of ferments, such as sauerkraut and pickled vegetables, which can be kept in large crocks or barrels at stable, cool temperatures for extended periods.

For fermented beverages like beer and wine, bottle storage in a cool, dark place is essential to prevent spoilage and maintain quality. Bottles should be kept on their sides to maintain the cork moist in the case of wine, which prevents air from entering and oxidizing the contents.

In conclusion, the selection of fermentation vessels and storage options is critical to the success and longevity of fermented products. Each vessel type offers unique benefits that cater to different fermentation needs, from small-batch home ferments in glass jars to large-scale commercial productions in stainless steel tanks. Proper storage, whether in a refrigerator, cellar, or specially designed bottles, ensures that fermented foods and beverages' delicious and healthful properties can be enjoyed well beyond the fermentation period. As interest in fermentation continues to grow, understanding the nuances of these containers and storage methods becomes an essential part of the fermenter's toolkit, enabling the creation of diverse and high-quality fermented goods.

## Common Fermented Foods in Prepping

In the realm of prepping, where the focus is on readiness for any situation, fermented foods hold a place of honor for their nutritional benefits, long shelf life, and flavor enhancement. Fermentation, one of the ancient food preservation methods, not only extends the usability of foods but also enriches them with probiotics, vitamins, and enzymes. This section delves into common fermented foods that are staples in prepping, discussing their benefits, preparation methods, and roles in ensuring food security and health during times of scarcity or emergency.

Sauerkraut, a fermented cabbage dish, is a prepper's ally due to its simplicity in preparation and robustness in nutrient content. Rich in vitamin C, digestive enzymes, and probiotics, sauerkraut is made by massaging salt into shredded cabbage and permitting it to ferment in its own juice under anaerobic conditions. This process fosters the growth of Lactobacillus bacteria, which not only preserves the cabbage but also turns it into a superfood. Its tangy flavor can complement a variety of dishes, making it a versatile addition to the prepper's pantry.

Kimchi, which is known as a staple in Korean cuisine, is another fermented vegetable dish highly regarded among preppers. Similar to sauerkraut but with a spicier kick and richer flavor profile, kimchi is made from cabbage and other vegetables mixed with a paste of garlic, ginger, and chili peppers. Fermentation enhances its nutritional value, introducing beneficial bacteria that promote gut health. Kimchi's longevity and the ease of making large batches make it an excellent option for stocking up.

Yogurt, a fermented dairy product, is prized for its high calcium levels, protein, and probiotics. Homemade yogurt is prepared by inoculating milk with specific yogurt cultures and allowing it to ferment at a warm temperature. The result is a creamy, nutritious food that can be consumed on its own or used as a base for smoothies and sauces. In a prepping context, yogurt can be made from powdered milk and stored in a cool place, offering a sustainable source of dairy.

Kefir, similar to yogurt but with a thinner consistency and a broader spectrum of probiotics, is another fermented dairy product ideal for preppers. Made by adding kefir grains to milk as well as allowing the mixture ferment, kefir can be consumed as a drink or used as a starter for other fermented foods. Its ease of preparation and the ability to reuse kefir grains make it a sustainable choice for long-term food planning.

While not a traditional "food" in the sense of being ready-to-eat upon fermentation, sourdough bread represents an essential aspect of prepping. The sourdough starter, a fermented mixture of water and flour, acts as a natural leavening agent. This starter can be maintained indefinitely with regular feeding, providing a reliable source of bread that doesn't rely on commercial yeast. Due to the fermentation process, sourdough bread's enhanced digestibility and nutritional profile make it a valuable staple for those looking to maximize the nutritional content of their stored grains.

Kombucha, a fermented tea beverage, is celebrated for its detoxifying properties and high levels of antioxidants. The fermentation is initiated by a SCOBY (symbiotic colony of bacteria and yeast), which metabolizes the sugar in the tea to produce a tangy, effervescent drink. Kombucha's popularity among preppers stems from its health benefits, including liver detoxification and immune system support, as well as its ability to be continuously brewed at home.

Miso, a Japanese seasoning made by fermenting the soybeans with salt and koji (a fungus), is a powerful addition to the prepper's food arsenal. Rich in protein, vitamins, and minerals, miso can be used to flavor soups, marinades, and sauces. Its long shelf life and dense nutritional profile make it an excellent item for long-term storage, providing essential nutrients and flavors to enhance various dishes.

In conclusion, fermented foods are invaluable in the context of prepping, offering a sustainable way to preserve food while enhancing its nutritional value and taste. From the tangy crunch of sauerkraut and kimchi to the creamy goodness of yogurt and kefir, the versatility of sourdough bread, the refreshing zing of kombucha, and the umami depth of miso, fermented foods cater to a wide range of dietary preferences and nutritional needs. Their preparation and storage require minimal resources, making them ideal for ensuring food security in uncertain times. Beyond their practical benefits, fermented foods also offer a connection to ancestral wisdom and the natural world, reminding us of the resilience and adaptability inherent in traditional food practices. As such, they represent not just a strategy for survival but a pathway to thriving, bringing flavor, health, and sustainability to the fore of prepping endeavors.

# CHAPTER VI

# Fermenting Vegetables

## Step-by-Step Guide to Lacto-Fermentation

Lacto-fermentation is a revered culinary practice that harnesses the natural process of fermentation to preserve and enhance foods' flavor and nutritional value. This ancient method, named for the lactic acid-producing bacteria involved, not only extends the shelf life of perishable items but also enriches them with probiotics, essential vitamins, and enzymes. In this section we will provide a comprehensive step-by-step guide to lacto-fermentation, detailing the preparation, fermentation, and storage processes to empower both novices and seasoned fermenters to explore the art of creating delicious, fermented foods at home.

The first step in lacto-fermentation is the selection of produce. Fresh, organic vegetables are ideal for fermentation as they are likely to have a higher microbial count, including the beneficial lactic acid bacteria necessary for fermentation. Popular choices include cabbage for sauerkraut, cucumbers for pickles, and carrots, beets, and radishes for flavored ferments. Ensuring the produce is fresh and free from blemishes or spoilage is crucial, as the ingredients' quality directly influences the fermentation's success.

Preparation of the produce follows, involving washing, chopping, grating, or slicing the vegetables to the desired size. This preparation step is essential for creating a uniform texture and size, which promotes even fermentation. For specific recipes, such as sauerkraut, massaging salt into the chopped cabbage is necessary to draw out water, creating a natural brine in which the fermentation will occur. The amount of salt used is critical, as it prevents the development of harmful bacteria while allowing lactobacillus bacteria to thrive. A general guideline is to use approximately 2-3% salt by weight of the prepared vegetables.

Once the produce is prepared and mixed with salt, it's time to pack it into fermentation vessels. Glass jars, ceramic crocks, or food-grade plastic containers can be used, provided they are clean and sterilized. The vegetables should be packed tightly into the vessels, eliminating air pockets and ensuring the produce is submerged under the brine. This anaerobic environment is vital for lacto-fermentation to occur. Weights or a smaller jar that is filled with water can be used to keep the vegetables submerged.

The fermentation vessel is then covered to protect the ferment from contaminants while allowing gases produced during fermentation to escape. A cloth cover secured with a rubber band or a specially designed airlock lid can be used for this purpose. The setup is then placed in a cool, dark location for the fermentation process to begin. The ideal temperature for lacto-fermentation is between 55°F to 75°F (13 degree Celcius to 24 degree Celcius), as temperatures outside this range can either slow down the fermentation or promote the growth of undesirable bacteria.

The duration of fermentation changes depending on the vegetable, temperature, and desired level of sourness. It can range from a few days to several weeks. During this time, checking the ferment regularly is essential, ensuring the vegetables remain submerged and observing any changes. Bubbles appearing on the surface, a tangy smell, and a change in texture are signs of successful fermentation.

Tasting the ferment at various stages can help determine when it has reached the intended flavor profile. Once satisfied, the fermented vegetables can be transferred to the refrigerator or a similarly cool place. This slows down the fermentation process, allowing the flavors to meld and mature over time. Refrigerated, lacto-fermented vegetables can last for several months, making them a convenient and nutritious addition to meals.

In conclusion, lacto-fermentation is a rewarding and accessible method for preserving and enhancing the nutritional value of vegetables. By following these steps— selecting quality produce, preparing and salting the vegetables, packing them into an anaerobic environment, and allowing the natural fermentation process to occur— anyone can create delicious, probiotic-rich foods. This guide to lacto-fermentation outlines the process's practical aspects and invites readers to partake in a culinary tradition that has nourished humans for millennia. As each batch of fermented vegetables is unique, the practice encourages experimentation and adaptation, offering endless possibilities for those willing to explore the art and science of fermentation.

## Recipes for Fermented Vegetables (e.g., Sauerkraut, Kimchi)

Fermented vegetables, which include sauerkraut and kimchi, are not only a scrumptious and tangy complement to meals, but they are also an abundant source of probiotics, vitamins, and enzymes. These traditional fermented foods have been eaten for ages and are lauded for their adaptability, the nutritional benefits they provide, and the bright tastes they possess. In this section, we will discuss recipes for two popular fermented vegetables, namely sauerkraut and kimchi. We will provide detailed directions that will walk readers through the process of preparing these delicacies that are rich in probiotics at home.

To produce sauerkraut, which is a mainstay in many European cuisines, cabbage is coarsely shredded and then subjected to lacto-fermentation. This process gives sauerkraut its distinctively acidic flavor and crunchy texture. In order to begin the process of making sauerkraut, you must first select a fresh head of cabbage and remove the outer leaves. The cabbage should be sliced very thinly, either by hand or with the use of a food processor, and then transferred to a medium-sized mixing bowl. It is recommended that you sprinkle salt over the shredded cabbage, using around one to one and a half tablespoons of salt for every pound of cabbage. Applying pressure to the cabbage with the salt until it begins to release its juices is the goal. It may take a few minutes to complete this process, but it is absolutely necessary in order to produce the brine that the cabbage will ferment in.

The cabbage should be packed securely into a clean fermentation vessel, which can be a glass jar or a ceramic crock, once it has released enough liquid to completely submerge itself during the fermentation process. It is important to make sure that the cabbage is completely submerged in the brine because it can become spoiled if it is exposed to air. If you want to keep the cabbage submerged, you can use a weight or a smaller jar that is filled with water. The fermenting jar should be covered with a clean cloth or lid, and there should be a rubber band used to secure it. Fermentation of the sauerkraut should take place for at least one to two weeks, depending on the desired level of sourness. The vessel should be placed in a cold, dark location with a temperature ranging from 55 degrees Fahrenheit to 75 degrees Fahrenheit (13 degrees Celsius to 24 degrees Celsius).

Kimchi, a meal that is considered to be an essential component of Korean cuisine, is a fermented vegetable dish that is commonly prepared using napa cabbage, radishes, and a number of different seasonings. The first step in making kimchi is to properly prepare the vegetables. The core of the napa cabbage should be removed before cutting it into quarters. It is important to ensure that the cabbage quarters are thoroughly rinsed in cold water, with the leaves being separated so that the brine can penetrate them. Allow the cabbage to sit for a few hours so that it can wilt, and then sprinkle salt throughout the leaves of the cabbage, paying particular attention to the thicker areas.

Garlic, ginger, Korean red pepper flakes (gochugaru), fish sauce, and a sweetener that includes sugar or honey should be blended together to make the kimchi paste. In the meantime, prepare the kimchi paste. You are free to vary the amounts of these components to suit your tastes in terms of flavor. For example, you might add more spice to make the kimchi more spicy, or you could add more sweetness to make it more mild. After it has wilted, the cabbage should be washed properly under cold water to eliminate any extra salt, and then it should be drained thoroughly.

Apply the kimchi paste to the cabbage leaves and any other veggies, such as radishes or carrots, and make sure that each individual piece is completely covered with the mixture. Pack the veggies that have been coated tightly into a fermentation vessel that has been thoroughly cleaned, pressing down firmly to remove any air pockets. To reiterate, make sure that the vegetables are completely submerged in the brine, and if required, use a weight or a smaller jar to do this. The kimchi should be allowed to ferment at room temperature between one to five days, depending on the desired level of fermentation and sourness. The vessel should be covered with a clean cloth or lid when the fermentation process begins.

As soon as the sauerkraut or kimchi has reached the level of fermentation that you wish, transfer it to jars that have been thoroughly cleaned and place it in the refrigerator. Vegetables that have been fermented will continue to acquire flavor over time; therefore, they can be consumed right away or left to mature for a few weeks for a more nuanced flavor. In addition to serving sauerkraut and kimchi as accompaniments to major dishes, you can also add them to salads or sandwiches to give them a tangy edge, or you may eat them on their own as healthful snacks. The power of fermentation can be harnessed by anyone looking to create homemade delicacies that are high in probiotics and are sure to thrill the taste senses while also providing nourishment to the body. These recipes are simple and easy to make.

## Troubleshooting Common Fermentation Issues

The process of fermentation is a time-honored culinary technique that is used to turn uncooked ingredients into foods that are both flavorful and healthful. In spite of the fact that the fermentation process is, for the most part, simple, there are a few problems that may crop up and have an impact on the final product of the fermentation. If you want to be sure that your batches of fermented foods are successful, it is vital to have a solid understanding of the frequent fermentation problems and how to solve them. Some of the most prevalent fermentation problems, such as mold growth, sluggish fermentation, off-flavors, and excessive gas production, are discussed in this section, along with some practical strategies to handle each of these difficulties.

It is possible that the formation of mold is one of the most serious difficulties that can arise throughout the fermentation process. There are certain molds that are not harmful, but there are also molds that can ruin the ferment and cause health problems. In most cases, the growth of mold takes place when the veggies are exposed to air or when they are not completely submerged in the brine. Make sure that all of the vegetables are completely submerged in the brine by pressing them down with weights or a smaller container. This will prevent the growth of mold throughout the brine process. Also, make sure to work in a clean area and utilize equipment that has been cleaned and disinfected. This will help reduce the amount of toxins that are introduced into the environment.

Fermenters may experience frustration when the fermentation process is sluggish, whether it is characterized by a lack of bubbling or slow development. This problem could be caused by a number of different circumstances, such as low temperatures, an inadequate amount of salt, or the consumption of vegetables that have a low level of microbial activity. If you are experiencing slow fermentation, you can try increasing the temperature of the fermentation environment to between 13 and 24 degrees Celsius (55 and 75 degrees Fahrenheit) in order to stimulate the activity of microorganisms. In addition, make sure that the appropriate quantity of salt is used, as salt serves as a natural preservative and contributes to the creation of an environment that is favorable to the fermentation process. In order to get the fermentation process off the ground, you might want to consider adding a starter culture or some whey from an earlier run of fermentation if you are utilizing veggies that have a low microbial activity.

There is a possibility that during the fermentation process, undesirable qualities, such as bitterness or an excessively sour taste, may emerge, which might diminish the overall enjoyment of the ferment. Inappropriate salt levels, excessive fermentation, or the presence of microorganisms that are not ideal can all contribute to the development of these off-flavors. Taste the ferment at regular intervals throughout the fermentation process in order to address any off-flavors that may be present. Adjust the salt levels or the fermentation time as necessary. If the ferment has an excessively sour or bitter flavor, it is probably preferable to throw it away and begin the process all over again with a fresh batch of veggies.

During the fermentation process, certain vegetables, like cabbage or beans, might produce an excessive amount of gas, which can lead to bloating or fermentation vessels that are on the verge of overflowing. This problem is often brought on by the emission of carbon dioxide gas throughout the fermentation process. This gas can accumulate if the ferment is packed too tightly or if there is not enough room for expansion. It is important to leave enough headroom at the top of the fermentation tank so that there is room for expansion and the release of gases. This will help prevent an excessive amount of gas generation. In addition, you should think about using an airlock lid or burping the ferment on a regular basis in order to remove the gas that has accumulated.

In conclusion, the ability to solve typical fermentation issues is a talent that is vital for fermenters of all levels. Fermenters are able to take preventative measures to address common concerns, such as mold growth, sluggish fermentation, off-flavors, and excessive gas production, by first gaining an understanding of the factors that take part to these problems. This allows them to ensure that batches of fermented foods are prepared successfully. Whether it's ensuring that vegetables are submerged correctly, adjusting salt levels, monitoring the progress of fermentation, or allowing for adequate gas release, the ability to troubleshoot fermentation issues gives fermenters the ability to create delicious as well as nutritious foods that are enjoyed for their flavor as well as the health benefits they provide. When fermenters put in the effort and have patience, they may overcome obstacles and become masters of the art of fermentation. This will allow them to open up a world of culinary possibilities and provide their bodies with delicacies that are rich in probiotics.

## Fermenting Vegetables in Various Environments

Fermenting vegetables is a varied and fulfilling culinary practice that may be adapted to a variety of settings, including the convenience of a home kitchen, outdoor settings, or even urban residences with limited space. Fermenting vegetables can be done in a variety of locations. The process of fermentation is dependent on the action of helpful microorganisms, especially lactic acid bacteria, which transform raw veggies into delights that are tart and high in probiotics. This section investigates the potential for fermenting vegetables in a variety of settings, focusing on the distinct difficulties and opportunities that are given by each habitat.

Fermenting vegetables is an easy technique that requires minimum equipment and can easily be included into daily activities. This process can be carried out in a regular home kitchen. As fermentation vessels, home fermenters often make use of glass jars, ceramic crocks, or food-grade plastic containers. Additionally, they incorporate fundamental kitchen utensils such as knives, cutting boards, and measuring spoons into their fermentation process. Because of its controlled atmosphere, which maintains consistent temperatures and allows for easy access to supplies, a kitchen is a perfect venue for fermenting vegetables throughout the whole year. For those who ferment their own food at home, they have the opportunity to experiment with a broad variety of recipes and flavors, ranging from traditional sauerkraut and kimchi to inventive combinations of vegetables, herbs, and spices.

Fermenting vegetables in an outdoor environment offers a number of distinct benefits, particularly for individuals who have access to outdoor space, such as a backyard or garden of their own. The use of outdoor fermenters allows for the utilization of natural sunlight and fresh air, both of which have the potential to stimulate the activity of microorganisms and improve the flavor of fermented foods. Fermenting larger amounts of vegetables, such as pickles or sauerkraut, can be accomplished with the use of huge ceramic crocks or wooden barrels. These containers still allow for enough air circulation and temperature control during the fermentation process. In addition, outdoor fermenters have the ability to use seasonal ingredients from their own garden or from the local farmers market, which can provide a sense of freshness and variety to their final products.

Despite the fact that space may be limited in urban contexts, it is still possible to ferment vegetables via inventiveness and resourcefulness. Urban fermenters may make use of fermentation vessels that are built for countertop usage, such as mason jars that are quart-sized or fermentation crocks that are designed for use on the countertop. Due to the fact that these compact vessels may be readily kept in kitchen cabinets or on shelves, they are an excellent choice for people who live in apartments or who have a limited amount of room in their kitchen. Alternative fermentation methods can also be explored by urban fermenters. These methods include lacto-fermenting vegetables in brine or fermenting in small batches with fermentation weights or airlocks to reduce the likelihood of the food going bad.

It is necessary to carefully prepare and pay attention to food safety requirements when fermenting vegetables on a bigger scale, whether the fermentation takes place in a commercial or community environment. In order to ferment vegetables in large numbers while adhering to stringent quality control standards, commercial fermenters may make use of specialist equipment, such as fermentation chambers or tanks made of stainless steel. Activities that involve communal fermentation, such as fermentation workshops or community-supported agriculture (CSA) programs, have the potential to bring people together for the purpose of gaining knowledge about fermentation processes, exchanging recipes, and providing support for local food systems.

Fermenting vegetables is a practice that can be applied to a variety of environments, including home kitchens, outdoor areas, urban flats, and commercial settings. It is a versatile and accessible method that gives you the ability to adapt to different circumstances. It is possible for fermenters to adjust their approach to fermentation to meet their own requirements and preferences if they have a thorough awareness of the specific obstacles and opportunities given by each setting. The art of fermentation provides a rich and exciting trip into the realm of probiotic-rich foods, culinary inventiveness, and sustainable food systems. This journey can be undertaken for the purpose of personal enjoyment, community participation, or commercial production of vegetables. Fermenters have the ability to harness the power of fermentation to change simple vegetables into complex and delectable delicacies that are both nourishing to the body and delighting to the senses. This can be accomplished with a little bit of experimenting and imaginative thinking.

# CHAPTER VII

# Fermenting Beverages

## Brewing Herbal Teas and Medicinal Infusions

Infusions of therapeutic herbs and teas are a time-honored ritual that has been passed down from generation to generation throughout cultures and civilizations, stretching back thousands of years. These beverages, which are made from a wide variety of herbs, flowers, roots, and spices, provide a wide range of flavors, smells, and health advantages. The preparation of herbal teas, which are often referred to as tisanes, involves steeping plant material in hot water. On the other hand, medical infusions are made by steeping the plant material for extended periods of time or by utilizing various procedures in order to extract powerful medicinal characteristics. This section dives into the art and science of making herbal teas and medicinal infusions, examining the vast array of botanicals that are available, the methods that are used to prepare them, and the health- promoting aspects that they offer.

When it comes to brewing herbal teas and medicinal infusions, one of the most enticing features is the incredible variety of botanical components that are available to pick from. Due to the fact that herbs like chamomile, peppermint, and lemon balm have relaxing and digestive properties, they are frequently used in teas that are consumed before going to bed or after meals. In addition to offering antioxidants and immune-boosting benefits, flowers such as hibiscus and elderflower are wonderful additions to teas since they impart beautiful colors and floral smells. Ginger and turmeric are two examples of roots that may be used to make infusions that are not only warming and spicy but also beneficial to digestion and reduce inflammation. Due to the wide variety of botanicals, tea fans are able to experiment endlessly, which enables them to create beverages that are tailored to their preferences as well as their health requirements.

Before beginning the process of brewing herbal teas and medicinal infusions, it is necessary to pick organic botanicals of the highest possible quality. Fresh or dried plant material, regardless of whether it comes from a garden, a local market, or a company with a good reputation, guarantees the highest possible flavor and potency. The method of brewing differs according to the outcome that wants to be achieved. When it comes to herbal teas, all that is required is to soak the herbs in hot water for five to ten minutes in order to extract their flavors and scents, resulting in a beverage that is both calming and pleasant. On the other hand, medicinal infusions can need to be steeped for longer periods of time or undergo additional processes, such as decoction (which involves heating herbs in water) or maceration (which involves soaking herbs in cold water or alcohol), in order to fully extract the medicinal characteristics of ingredients.

When boiling herbal teas and medicinal infusions, temperature and the amount of time spent steeping are two of the most important aspects. In order to acquire the proper flavor and strength, various botanicals require heating at different temperatures and for varying amounts of time. When using delicate herbs such as chamomile and mint, it is recommended to steep them in water that has been brought to a low boil, after which the water should be allowed to gently cool down before being poured over the herbs. Ginger and cinnamon are examples of heartier herbs that are able to survive higher temperatures and longer steeping durations without succumbing to bitterness or becoming overbearing. Tea fans are able to fine-tune their brews to their preferences by experimenting with temperature and steeping duration. This allows them to choose whether they want a light and refreshing infusion or a bold and robust herbal tea.

There are an array of health advantages that can be derived from herbal teas and medicinal infusions, just like the botanicals themselves. An abundance of herbs contain phytochemicals, antioxidants, and essential oils, all of which contribute to the general health and well-being of the individual. For example, chamomile has been utilized for years as a natural therapy for insomnia and anxiety, and ginger is highly regarded for its anti-inflammatory and digestive characteristics. Both of these remedies have been used for generations. Both peppermint and lemon balm are well-known for their capacity to calm stomachs that are disturbed and to alleviate nausea, which makes them ideal assets to any home apothecary. Individuals can harness the healing power of plants to boost vitality and resilience by introducing herbal teas and medicinal infusions into their everyday routines. This involves incorporating these beverages into their routines.

Creating herbal teas and medicinal infusions is a wonderful and beneficial exercise that encourages inquiry, creativity, and a connection to the natural world. In conclusion, this practice is a delightful and healthful activity. Everyone can find something to their liking in the world of herbal beverages, whether they are looking for relaxation, rejuvenation, or relief from common ailments. The world of herbal beverages includes everything from fragrant floral blends to spicy, warming infusions. It is possible for individuals to acquire a deeper appreciation for the curative power of plants and begin on a path of wellness and self-discovery by selecting botanicals of high quality, experimenting with different brewing processes, and appreciating the many flavors and benefits of herbal teas and infusions.

## Making Fermented Drinks (e.g., Kombucha, Kvass)

The production of fermented beverages, including kombucha and kvass, is a process that dates back hundreds of years and has experienced a rising level of popularity in recent years. A tasty way to improve gut health, boost immunity, and satisfy thirst, these beverages are loaded with probiotics and offer a variety of benefits. A sweetened tea is fermented with a symbiotic culture of bacteria and yeast (SCOBY) in order to produce kombucha, a tea-based beverage that is characterized by its sourness and carbonation. As a result of the fermentation process, the sugar and tea are transformed into a beverage that is sour and somewhat carbonated, and the bacterial content of the beverage is responsible for a wide range of health advantages. On the other hand, kvass is a traditional beverage from the Slavic region that is produced by fermenting bread or grains. Typically, it has a moderately acidic taste, and it can be flavored with anything from fruits and vegetables to herbs. Kombucha and kvass are two beverages that, despite their variations in ingredients and origins, have a lot in common with one another, including the fermentation process and the health-promoting benefits that they possess.

Begin the process of making kombucha by brewing a batch of sweetened tea using either black tea, green tea, or even a combination of the two types of tea. It is time to add the SCOBY to the tea once it has reached room temperature. Additionally, some starter liquid from a previous batch of kombucha should be added in order to initiate the fermentation process. The SCOBY, which is frequently referred to as the "mother," is a culture that resembles a rubbery disk and floats on the top of the tea.

It is the organism that is responsible for fermenting the sugars into organic acids and gases. The fermentation process should be allowed to continue for seven to fourteen days, depending on the desired level of tartness and fizziness. Make sure to cover the brewing vessel with a clean cloth or paper towel to prevent impurities from entering while yet allowing ventilation.

The fermentation process for kvass, on the other hand, begins with stale bread or grains that are steeped in water and allowed to ferment for a number of working days. During the fermentation process, the starches in the bread or grains are broken down into sugars. These sugars are subsequently transformed into alcohol and carbon dioxide by bacteria and wild yeast that are present in the environment. Immediately following the completion of the fermentation process, the liquid is filtered and flavored with various components, such fruits, vegetables, or herbs, before being bottled and stored in the refrigerator. In addition to being consumed on its own as a refreshing beverage, kvass can also be utilized as a foundation for soups and sauces.

Both kombucha and kvass are sources of several health advantages, which can be attributed to the fermentation process and the presence of probiotics in both beverages. Beneficial bacteria known as probiotics are known to strengthen digestive health, boost the immune system, and possibly even have an effect on mood. It is also important to note that fermented beverages such as kombucha and kvass are abundant in organic acids, vitamins, and antioxidants, all of which contribute to the health benefits that these beverages offer. The drinking of these beverages on a consistent basis may assist to improve digestion, boost the absorption of nutrients, and support general well-being through their consumption.

In addition to the positive effects that they have on one's health, fermented beverages such as kombucha and kvass can be a leisure activity that is both enjoyable and fulfilling. Homebrewers have the ability to produce one-of-a-kind and individualized beverages that are tailored to their preferences and tastes by experimenting with various tea blends, flavor combinations, and fermentation procedures. A deeper connection to the natural world and the cycles of fermentation is fostered via the process of brewing kombucha and kvass. Additionally, the process provides a sense of satisfaction and success with each batch that is prepared.

In conclusion, the production of fermented beverages such as kombucha and kvass provides a delectable and nourishing method to promote the health of the digestive tract, strengthen the immune system, and investigate the realm of fermentation. Whether they ferment kvass with stale bread or brew kombucha with a SCOBY, homebrewers have the opportunity to reap the advantages of the probiotics, organic acids, and antioxidants that are present in these traditional beverages. The art of preparing fermented drinks at home is something that can be mastered by anyone with a little bit of patience and experimenting. This might open up a whole new world of flavor, health, and creativity for an individual.


## Exploring Alcoholic Fermentation (e.g., Mead, Fruit Wines)

Exploring alcoholic fermentation, through beverages such as mead and fruit wines, is a journey that taps into tradition and innovation. Alcoholic fermentation, a natural process driven by yeast converting sugars into alcohol and carbon dioxide, has been practiced by humans for millennia. Mead, often called the "nectar of the gods," is one of the ancient known alcoholic beverages, made from fermenting honey with water and sometimes flavored with fruits, herbs, or spices. On the other hand, fruit wines are made from fermenting the sugars present in various fruits, such as grapes, berries, apples, and pears. These beverages offer diverse flavors, aromas, and characteristics, making them beloved by enthusiasts and connoisseurs alike.

Mead-making begins with selecting high-quality honey, which serves as the primary fermentable sugar. Different types of honey, which includes wildflower, clover, or orange blossom, can impart unique flavors and aromas to the finished mead. The honey is diluted with water to achieve the desired sweetness and gravity, and sometimes supplemented with fruits, spices, or herbs to add complexity and depth. Once the ingredients are combined, yeast is added to kickstart the fermentation process. Fermentation can take from several weeks to several months, depending on factors which includes temperature, yeast strain, and desired alcohol content. The result is a sweet, dry, or semi-sweet beverage with many flavors, from floral and fruity to spicy and earthy.

Fruit wines, like mead, offer endless possibilities for creativity and experimentation. Grapes are perhaps the most well-known fruit used in winemaking, with varietals such as Cabernet Sauvignon, Chardonnay, and Merlot dominating the market. However, other fruits can also be used to make delicious wines, including berries like strawberries, raspberries, and blackberries, as well as apples, pears, peaches, and plums. Each fruit imparts its unique flavor profile, acidity, and sweetness to the wine, resulting in diverse styles and expressions. The winemaking process involves crushing or pressing the fruit to extract the juice, and then it is fermented with yeast to transform the sugars into alcohol. Fermentation may take weeks to months, followed by aging in oak barrels and/or stainless steel tanks to develop complexity and character.

One of the joys of exploring alcoholic fermentation is the opportunity to experiment with different ingredients, techniques, and styles. Homebrewers and winemakers can tailor their recipes to suit their preferences, whether they prefer dry, sweet, sparkling, or still beverages. Additionally, the process of fermentation itself can be an art form, with careful attention paid to factors such as yeast selection, fermentation temperature, and aging conditions to achieve desired outcomes. Whether making mead with local honey and wildflower botanicals or fermenting fruit wines with freshly picked berries from the garden, the possibilities are limited only by one's imagination and creativity.

Beyond the pleasure of crafting and enjoying these beverages, alcoholic fermentation offers numerous benefits, both culinary and cultural. Mead and fruit wines have been enjoyed by cultures around the world for centuries, playing integral roles in religious rituals, celebrations, and social gatherings. They are also valued for their probable health benefits when consumed in moderation, including antioxidant properties, heart health benefits, and potential immune-boosting effects. Moreover, the process of fermentation itself is a natural and sustainable way to preserve and transform raw ingredients into flavorful and shelf-stable beverages, reducing food waste and supporting local agriculture.

In conclusion, exploring alcoholic fermentation through beverages like mead and fruit wines is a fascinating and rewarding endeavor that combines tradition, innovation, and craftsmanship. Whether delving into the ancient art of mead-making or experimenting with fruit wines, enthusiasts can embark on a journey of discovery, creativity, and enjoyment. With a deep appreciation for the natural world, an adventurous spirit, and a willingness to experiment, anyone can unlock the secrets of alcoholic fermentation and savor the fruits of their labor. Cheers to the endless possibilities of fermentation and its delightful beverages.

## Safety Precautions in Brewing and Fermenting Beverages

Safety precautions in brewing and fermenting beverages are paramount to ensure the brewer's and consumers' health and well-being. While brewing and fermenting beverages can be a rewarding and enjoyable hobby, it also involves working with microorganisms, handling potentially hazardous chemicals, and creating an environment conducive to microbial growth. By implementing proper safety measures, brewers can minimize the risk of contamination, spoilage, and injury, while producing high-quality and safe beverages for consumption.

Maintaining a clean and sanitized workspace is one of the most critical safety precautions in brewing and fermenting beverages. Proper sanitation helps to prevent the growth of harmful bacteria, yeast, and mold, which can spoil the batch and pose health risks. Brewers should thoroughly clean and sanitize all equipment, utensils, and surfaces before and after each use, using food-grade sanitizers or cleaning solutions. This includes fermenters, brewing vessels, airlocks, tubing, bottles, and caps. Additionally, brewers should practice good personal hygiene, including washing hands frequently, wearing clean clothing, and avoiding cross-contamination between raw ingredients and finished products.

Another essential safety consideration is working with ingredients and additives responsibly. Brewers should use high-quality ingredients from reputable sources, ensuring they are free from contaminants, pesticides, and any other harmful substances. When handling ingredients such as hops, grains, fruit, or herbs, brewers should wear appropriate protective gear, which includes gloves and eye protection, to prevent skin irritation or injury. It's also essential to store ingredients properly in a cool, dry, as well as well-ventilated area to maintain freshness and to avoid spoilage.

Proper handling and storage of fermentation vessels and equipment are also crucial for ensuring safety in brewing and fermenting beverages. Fermentation vessels should be made of food-grade materials, such as stainless steel, glass, or food-grade plastic, to avoid leaching of harmful chemicals into the brew. Brewers should inspect vessels and equipment for signs of wear, damage, or corrosion, and replace or repair as needed to prevent accidents or contamination. Additionally, fermenters should be equipped with airlocks or blow-off tubes to allow gases produced during fermentation to escape safely without exposing the brew to oxygen or contaminants.

Temperature control is another important safety consideration in brewing and fermenting beverages, mainly when working with live cultures such as yeast and bacteria. Fermentation temperature plays a critical part in the activity and viability of these microorganisms, with optimal ranges varying depending on the specific strain and style of beverage being brewed. Brewers should carefully monitor and control fermentation temperatures, using methods such as temperature-controlled fermentation chambers, fermentation wraps, or water baths to maintain stability and consistency. Fluctuations in temperature can lead to off-flavors, sluggish fermentation, or contamination, compromising the safety and quality of the final product.

Lastly, proper handling and disposal of waste and byproducts are essential safety precautions in brewing and fermenting beverages. Brewers should responsibly dispose of spent grains, hops, yeast, and other brewing residues, following local regulations and guidelines for waste management. This may include composting organic waste, recycling packaging materials, and properly disposing of hazardous chemicals or cleaning agents. Brewers can contribute to a more sustainable and eco-friendly brewing process by minimizing waste and reducing environmental impact.

In conclusion, safety precautions are paramount in brewing and fermenting beverages to ensure the health and safety of both the brewer and the consumers. By maintaining a clean and sanitized workspace, handling ingredients responsibly, properly storing equipment, controlling fermentation temperatures, and disposing of waste properly, brewers can minimize the risk of contamination, spoilage, and injury, while producing high-quality and safe beverages for enjoyment. Whether brewing beer, fermenting wine, or crafting kombucha, prioritizing safety is necessary for a successful and enjoyable brewing experience.

# CHAPTER VIII

# Fermenting Dairy and Grains

## Culturing Yogurt and Kefir

Culturing yogurt and kefir is a fascinating and rewarding process that allows individuals to create delicious and nutritious fermented dairy products at home. Both yogurt and kefir are traditional dairy foods that have been consumed for centuries, prized for their probiotic content, creamy texture, and tangy flavor. While yogurt is made by fermenting milk with specific strains of lactic acid bacteria, kefir is a fermented milk drink that is created by inoculating milk with kefir grains, a symbiotic culture of bacteria and yeast. This section explores the art and science of culturing yogurt and kefir, from selecting high-quality ingredients to fermenting and enjoying the finished products.

The first step in culturing yogurt and kefir is selecting high-quality milk. Whether using cow's milk, goat's milk, or plant-based alternatives which includes coconut milk or almond milk, it's essential to choose fresh, pasteurized milk free from additives or preservatives. The milk's quality directly impacts the final product's flavor, texture, and nutritional value, so opt for organic or locally sourced milk whenever possible. The milk is heated for yogurt to kill harmful bacteria and denature the proteins, then cooled to a specific temperature before inoculating with yogurt culture. For kefir, the milk is simply combined with kefir grains, which contain a diverse community of bacteria and yeast responsible for fermentation.

Once the milk is prepared, it's time to inoculate it with the appropriate culture. This involves adding a small amount of yogurt starter culture containing live bacteria strains such as Lactobacillus bulgaricus as well as Streptococcus thermophilus. These bacteria ferment the lactose that is present in the milk, developing lactic acid, which thickens the milk and gives yogurt its characteristic tangy flavor. For kefir, the milk is inoculated with kefir grains, which contain a mixture of lactic acid bacteria, acetic acid bacteria, and yeast. These microorganisms ferment the lactose and other sugars in the milk, producing carbon dioxide gas and alcohol, which give kefir its effervescent texture and slightly sour taste.

The fermentation process for yogurt and kefir typically takes between 12 to 24 hours, based on factors such as temperature, milk type, and desired thickness. During fermentation, the live bacteria and yeast in the culture metabolize the sugars in the milk, producing lactic acid, acetic acid, and other compounds that take part to the final product's flavor, texture, and nutritional profile. For yogurt, the milk is incubated at a warm temperature (around 110°F to 115°F or 43°C to 46°C) to encourage bacterial growth and fermentation. For kefir, the milk is typically fermented at room temperature, allowing the kefir grains to culture the milk over a longer period.

Once the yogurt and kefir have reached the desired level of fermentation, they can be chilled in the refrigerator to halt the fermentation process and set the texture. The yogurt will have thickened and developed a tangy flavor, while the kefir will have a creamy texture with a slight fizziness and tanginess. Both yogurt and kefir can be enjoyed plain or flavored with additions such as fruit, honey, nuts, or spices to create a variety of delicious and nutritious snacks, desserts, or beverages. Additionally, yogurt and kefir can be used in cooking and baking, adding richness, flavor, and probiotic benefits to a wide range of dishes.

Beyond their delicious taste and creamy texture, yogurt and kefir offer numerous health benefits thanks to their probiotic content. Probiotics are known as beneficial bacteria that support digestive health, boost immunity, and may even have mood-enhancing effects. Regular consumption of yogurt and kefir has been linked to improved digestion, reduced inflammation, enhanced nutrient absorption, and a lower risk of certain chronic diseases. Additionally, yogurt and kefir are rich in protein, calcium, vitamins, and minerals, making them valuable additions to a balanced diet.

In conclusion, culturing yogurt and kefir at home is a rewarding and enjoyable process that allows individuals to create delicious and nutritious fermented dairy products. Anyone can enjoy the benefits of homemade yogurt and kefir by selecting high-quality ingredients, inoculating with the appropriate cultures, and fermenting at the right temperature. Whether enjoyed plain, flavored, or used as ingredients in cooking and baking, yogurt and kefir offer a versatile and delicious way to incorporate probiotics into one's diet and support overall health and well-being. With a little time, patience, and creativity, anyone can master the art of culturing yogurt and kefir and enjoy their many delights.

## Making Fermented Cheeses

Making fermented cheeses is a centuries-old craft that combines science, artistry, and tradition to produce a diverse array of delicious and complex dairy products. From creamy Brie to sharp cheddar, fermented cheeses are beloved for their rich flavors, unique textures, and culinary versatility. Making fermented cheeses involves inoculating milk with specific strains of bacteria and/or mold cultures, allowing the milk to ferment and curdle, draining the whey, pressing and aging the curds, and finally, enjoying the finished cheese. This section explores the intricate steps involved in making fermented cheeses, from selecting high-quality milk to aging the cheese to perfection.

The first step in making fermented cheeses is selecting high-quality milk. Fresh, pasteurized milk from cows, goats, sheep, or buffalo serves as the base ingredient for cheese-making. The quality and composition of the milk directly impact the flavor, texture, and quality of the final cheese, so it's essential to choose milk free from additives, antibiotics, and hormones. Many cheese-makers prefer to use raw milk, as it has a natural enzymes and beneficial bacteria that contribute to the fermentation and aging process. However, pasteurized milk can also be used successfully, provided it is of high quality and freshness.

Once the milk is selected, it's time to inoculate it with specific strains of bacteria and/or mold cultures to kickstart the fermentation process. Different cheeses require different combinations of cultures to achieve their desired flavor, texture, and aroma. For example, lactic acid bacteria such as Lactococcus, Lactobacillus, and Streptococcus are commonly used to acidify the milk and produce the characteristic tangy flavor of cheeses like Cheddar and Gouda. Other cheeses, such as blue cheeses like Roquefort and Gorgonzola, require the addition of mold cultures such as Penicillium roqueforti or Penicillium glaucum to develop their distinctive blue veins and complex flavors.

After inoculating the milk with cultures, rennet or another coagulating agent is added to curdle the milk and form curds. Rennet contains enzymes that help break down the proteins in the milk, which cause it to coagulate and form a gel-like mass of curds. The curds are then cut into small pieces to release whey, the liquid portion of the milk. The size and shape of the curds vary depending on the desired texture of the cheese, with larger curds producing a softer cheese and smaller curds producing a firmer cheese. The curds are compacted and shaped further by pressing them into molds after the whey is drained off.

Once the curds are pressed, the cheese is ready for aging. Aging is known as a critical step in the cheese-making process, as it allows the flavors and textures of the cheese to develop and mature over time. During aging, the cheese is stored in a temperature- and humidity-controlled environment, such as a cheese cave or aging room, where it is exposed to specific conditions that encourage microbial activity and enzymatic breakdown of proteins and fats. This process results in changes to the flavor, texture, and appearance of the cheese, with other cheeses aged for just a few weeks and others aged for months or even years to achieve their desired characteristics.

Throughout the aging process, cheese-makers carefully monitor and tend to their cheeses, flipping and brushing them to ensure even ripening and prevent the growth of unwanted molds or bacteria. Some cheeses, such as washed-rind cheeses like Munster and Taleggio, are periodically washed or rubbed with brine, beer, or other solutions to encourage the growth of desirable bacteria and molds on the surface of the cheese, which contribute to their unique flavors and aromas.

Finally, once the cheese has reached its intended level of maturity, it is ready to be enjoyed. Fermented cheeses offer a wide range of flavors, textures, and aromas, from mild and creamy to sharp and pungent, catering to various tastes and preferences. Whether served on a cheese platter, melted into a sauce, or crumbled over a salad, fermented cheeses add depth and richness to countless dishes and culinary creations.

In conclusion, making fermented cheeses is a time-honored craft that combines science, artistry, and tradition to produce a diverse array of delicious and complex dairy products. From selecting high-quality milk to inoculating with specific cultures, coagulating, pressing, aging, and finally, enjoying the finished cheese, each step in the cheese-making process requires skill, patience, and attention to detail. Whether made in small artisanal batches or produced on a larger commercial scale, fermented cheeses represent the culmination of centuries of cheese-making tradition and expertise, offering a taste of culinary history and culture with every bite.

## Fermenting Grains for Breads and Porridges

Fermenting grains for breads and porridges is a time-honored strategy that dates back thousands of years and spans cultures worldwide. Fermentation enhances the flavor and texture of grains and unlocks their nutritional potential by breaking down anti-nutrients and increasing bioavailability of vitamins and minerals. From sourdough bread to fermented porridges like idli and injera, fermented grains play a central role in global cuisines, offering diverse flavors, aromas, and health benefits. This section delves into the art and science of fermenting grains for breads and porridges, exploring the fermentation process, its benefits, and its culinary applications.

Fermenting begins with selecting high-quality grains, such as wheat, rye, barley, oats, rice, or corn. Whole grains are preferred, as they retain their natural bran, germ, and endosperm, which contain essential nutrients like fiber, protein, vitamins, and minerals. The grains are then soaked, sprouted, or ground into flour prior being mixed with water to create a dough or batter. Next, a fermenting agent, such as wild yeast from a sourdough starter or a specific strain of bacteria, is added to the dough to initiate fermentation. The fermenting agent metabolizes the carbohydrates in the grains, producing carbon dioxide gas and organic acids, which leaven the dough and impart a tangy flavor.

Sourdough bread is one of the most popular and well-known examples of fermented grains. Sourdough bread is created by fermenting a combination of flour and also water with wild yeast and lactobacilli bacteria present in a sourdough starter. The sourdough starter, also known as levain or mother dough, is a mixture of flour and water that has been fermented over several days or several weeks to cultivate a stable population of wild yeast and lactobacilli bacteria. When mixed with fresh flour and water, the sourdough starter inoculates the dough with its microbial community, ferments the flour's carbohydrates, produces carbon dioxide gas, and leavens the bread.

Fermented grains are also used to make a variety of porridges, including idli, dosa, injera, and amazake. Idli and dosa are traditional South Indian dishes made from fermented rice as well as lentil batter, which is steamed or cooked on a griddle to make soft, fluffy cakes or crispy pancakes, respectively. Injera is known as a staple food in Ethiopia and Eritrea made from fermented teff flour batter, which is poured onto a hot griddle and cooked into a spongy, slightly sour flatbread. Amazake is a traditional Japanese sweet fermented rice drink made by fermenting cooked rice with koji mold, which breaks down the starches in the rice into simple sugars, resulting in a sweet, creamy beverage.

The fermentation of grains offers numerous benefits, both culinary and nutritional. Fermentation improves the digestibility of grains by breaking down intricate carbohydrates, proteins, and fats into simpler compounds that are easier for the body to absorb. It also increases the bioavailability of vitamins as well as minerals, such as B vitamins, iron, and zinc, making them more accessible and nutritious. Additionally, fermentation enhances grains' flavor, aroma, and texture, imparting a pleasant tanginess, depth, and complexity to breads, porridges, and other fermented grain products.

Furthermore, fermenting grains is a sustainable and eco-friendly practice that reduces food waste and enhances food security. By fermenting grains, individuals can extend the shelf life of perishable ingredients, reducing the need for preservatives and additives. Fermented grains can also be stored for longer periods without spoiling, providing a reliable source of nutrition year-round. Additionally, fermenting grains can help preserve traditional culinary techniques and cultural heritage, fostering a deeper appreciation for the rich diversity of fermented grain foods worldwide.

In conclusion, fermenting grains for breads and porridges is a time-honored tradition that offers numerous culinary, nutritional, and cultural benefits. From sourdough bread to fermented porridges like idli and injera, fermented grains play a central role in global cuisines, providing diverse flavors, textures, and health benefits. By fermenting grains, individuals can unlock the nutritional potential of grains, enhance their digestibility, and create delicious and nutritious foods that nourish the body and soul. With a deep appreciation for the art and science of fermentation, anyone can harness the power of grains to create a world of flavorful and nutritious delights.

## Incorporating Fermented Dairy and Grains into Survival Recipes

Incorporating fermented dairy and grains into survival recipes is a practical approach to food preservation and a way to enhance nutrition, flavor, and variety in emergencies. Fermented dairy products which includes yogurt, kefir, and cheese, along with fermented grains such as sourdough bread, provide essential nutrients, probiotics, and sustained energy, making them valuable additions to survival diets. Whether facing natural disasters, long-term emergencies, or wilderness survival scenarios, understanding how to incorporate fermented dairy and grains into survival recipes can help individuals maintain their health, resilience, and morale during challenging times.

One of the primary benefits of incorporating fermented dairy and grains into survival recipes is their long shelf life and resilience to spoilage. Fermented dairy products which includes yogurt and kefir can be kept for extended periods without refrigeration, thanks to their acidic pH and beneficial bacteria that inhibit the growth of harmful pathogens. Similarly, fermented grains like sourdough bread have a longer shelf life than conventional bread due to the fermentation process, which increases acidity and reduces moisture content, making them less susceptible to mold and spoilage. By including these fermented foods in survival kits or emergency supplies, individuals can ensure access to nutritious and reliable sources of sustenance during prolonged periods of hardship or scarcity.

Another advantage of fermented dairy and grains in survival recipes is their nutritional density and versatility. Fermented dairy products which includes yogurt, kefir, and cheese are rich in protein, calcium, vitamins, and probiotics, which support overall health and well-being. They can be consumed on their own or used as ingredients in various survival recipes, from savory stews and soups to hearty sandwiches and wraps. Similarly, fermented grains like sourdough bread provide complex carbohydrates, fiber, and essential nutrients, making them a valuable source of sustained energy and satiety in survival situations. Whether eaten as a standalone meal or paired with other foods, fermented dairy and grains offer a convenient and nutritious option for individuals navigating challenging circumstances.

Moreover, incorporating fermented dairy and grains into survival recipes can help improve digestion and gut health, which is crucial for maintaining immunity and resilience during emergencies. Fermented dairy products which includes yogurt and kefir contain probiotics, helpful bacteria that promote a healthy gut flora balance and support digestive function. Consuming these probiotic-rich foods can help alleviate digestive discomfort, prevent gastrointestinal infections, and enhance nutrient absorption, particularly in situations where access to fresh fruits and vegetables may be limited. Similarly, fermented grains like sourdough bread contain prebiotics, which act as food for probiotic bacteria in the gut, further supporting digestive health and overall well-being.

In addition to their nutritional and digestive benefits, fermented dairy and grains offer culinary diversity and flavor enhancement in survival recipes. Fermented dairy products which includes yogurt, kefir, and cheese add tanginess, creaminess, and depth of flavor to an array of dishes, from simple salads and dips to complex curries and casseroles. Similarly, fermented grains like sourdough bread provide a distinct sourdough flavor and chewy texture that can elevate sandwiches, toast, and baked goods. By incorporating these fermented foods into survival recipes, individuals can enjoy a greater variety of flavors and textures, enhancing their meals' overall enjoyment and satisfaction during challenging times.

Furthermore, learning how to ferment dairy and grains at home gives individuals valuable skills and knowledge that can be applied in numerous survival scenarios. In situations where access to commercial food sources may be limited or unreliable, knowing how to ferment dairy and grains allows individuals to produce their own nutritious and shelf-stable foods using minimal equipment and resources. With essential ingredients like milk, water, flour, and salt, individuals can create homemade yogurt, kefir, cheese, and sourdough bread, providing a sustainable and self-sufficient source of nourishment in times of need.

In conclusion, incorporating fermented dairy and grains into survival recipes is a practical and effective strategy for enhancing nutrition, flavor, and resilience in emergencies. Fermented dairy products which includes yogurt, kefir, and cheese, along with fermented grains like sourdough bread, offer long shelf lives, nutritional density, digestive benefits, and culinary versatility, making them valuable additions to survival diets. By including these fermented foods in emergency supplies and learning how to ferment dairy and grains at home, individuals can ensure access to nutritious and reliable sources of sustenance during times of hardship or uncertainty. With a focus on preparedness, resourcefulness, and adaptability, anyone can harness the power of fermented dairy and grains to thrive in survival scenarios.

# CHAPTER IX

# Long-Term Storage and Preservation

## Proper Storage Containers for Pickled and Fermented Foods

Proper storage containers for pickled and fermented foods are crucial for maintaining their quality, flavor, and safety over time. Whether fermenting vegetables like sauerkraut or pickling cucumbers for crunchy dill pickles, choosing the right containers ensures that the fermentation process proceeds smoothly and that the final products remain fresh and flavorful. In this section, we will explore the importance of proper storage containers for pickled and fermented foods, as well as the characteristics to consider when choosing containers for different types of ferments.

Material composition is one of the most critical factors to consider when selecting storage containers for pickled and fermented foods. Containers made of food-grade materials such as glass, ceramic, or stainless steel are ideal choices as they are non-reactive and non-porous. This means they won't absorb odors, flavors, or harmful chemicals that could have an effect on the quality of the ferments. Glass jars, in particular, are popular for fermenting vegetables and pickles because they are transparent, allowing for easy monitoring of the fermentation process. Additionally, glass jars can be sealed tightly with a lid to prevent exposure to oxygen and contaminants, creating an ideal environment for fermentation to occur.

Size and shape are other important considerations when choosing storage containers for pickled and fermented foods. Containers should be large enough to accommodate the amount of food being fermented while leaving enough headspace to expand gases produced during fermentation. Wide-mouth jars or crocks are often preferred for fermenting vegetables, as they provide easy access for packing and removing the vegetables. Additionally, wide-mouth jars allow for the use of weights or fermentation lids to submerge the vegetables in brine or liquid, which helps prevent spoilage and contamination. Containers with straight sides are also easier to clean and sanitize than those with narrow necks or irregular shapes.

In addition to material composition and size, ventilation and anaerobic conditions are essential considerations when selecting storage containers for pickled and fermented foods. Fermentation is known as an anaerobic process, meaning it occurs without oxygen. Therefore, containers should be airtight or equipped with airlocks to prevent the entry of oxygen, which can result in spoilage or the growth of harmful bacteria and mold. Fermentation lids or airlocks allow carbon dioxide produced during fermentation to escape while avoiding oxygen from entering the container, creating an ideal environment for fermentation to occur.

When it comes to storing fermented foods long-term, such as sauerkraut, kimchi, or pickles, temperature and light exposure are additional factors to consider. Fermented foods should be stored in a cool, dark place, away from direct sunlight as well as extreme temperatures. Exposure to light and heat can increase spoilage and degrade the quality of the ferments, leading to off-flavors and textural changes. Pantry shelves, root cellars, or refrigerators are all suitable storage locations for fermented foods, depending on the type of ferment and the desired shelf life. Some ferments, such as sourdough starter or kefir grains, may benefit from being stored in the refrigerator to slow fermentation and extend their lifespan.

Furthermore, ease of cleaning and maintenance is an important consideration when choosing storage containers for pickled and fermented foods. Containers should be easy to disassemble, clean, and sanitize between uses to prevent the buildup of harmful bacteria or mold. Glass jars and ceramic crocks are dishwasher-safe and can be sanitized using hot water and soap or by boiling them in water for a few minutes. Stainless steel containers are also simple to clean and sanitize, making them suitable for fermenting foods that may require higher levels of hygiene, such as dairy or meat ferments.

In conclusion, proper storage containers are essential for preserving pickled and fermented foods' quality, flavor, and safety. When choosing containers for fermentation, it's critical to consider factors which includes material composition, size and shape, ventilation, anaerobic conditions, temperature and light exposure, and ease of cleaning and maintenance. Glass jars, ceramic crocks, and stainless steel containers are popular choices for fermenting vegetables, pickles, and other fermented foods, as they provide an ideal environment for fermentation to occur. By selecting the right containers and following proper storage practices, individuals can enjoy delicious and nutritious fermented foods that are safe and enjoyable to eat.

## Techniques for Extending Shelf Life

Extending the shelf life of pickled and fermented foods is essential for preserving their quality, flavor, and nutritional value over time. Whether fermenting vegetables like sauerkraut or pickling cucumbers for crunchy dill pickles, employing proper techniques can help ensure that these delicious and nutritious foods remain safe and enjoyable to eat for longer periods. In this section, we will explore various techniques for extending the shelf life of pickled and fermented foods, including proper fermentation, storage, packaging, and preservation methods.

One of the most effective techniques for extending the shelf life of pickled and fermented foods is ensuring proper fermentation during the initial processing stage. Fermentation is a natural preservation method that relies on the activity of helpful microorganisms, such as lactic acid bacteria, to acidify and preserve foods. By controlling factors such as temperature, salt concentration, and fermentation time, fermenters can create an environment conducive to the development of beneficial bacteria while inhibiting the development of harmful bacteria and mold. Proper fermentation not only preserves the texture, flavor, and nutritional content of the foods but also creates a natural barrier against spoilage and contamination.

Another technique for extending the shelf life of pickled and fermented foods is proper storage and packaging. Fermented foods should be stored in clean, airtight containers made of food-grade materials such as glass, ceramic, or stainless steel. These containers should be stored in a cool, dark place, away from direct sunlight as well as extreme temperatures, which can accelerate spoilage and degrade the quality of the ferments. Additionally, fermented foods should be stored at the appropriate temperature for optimal preservation, whether in the pantry, refrigerator, or freezer, depending on the type of ferment and desired shelf life.

Vacuum sealing is another effective packaging technique for extending the shelf life of pickled and fermented foods. Vacuum sealing removes air from the packaging, creating a vacuum environment that slows down the development of spoilage organisms and oxidation, which can degrade the quality of the foods. Vacuum-sealed bags or jars can be used to store fermented foods such as sauerkraut, kimchi, and pickles, extending their shelf life by weeks or even months compared to traditional storage methods. Vacuum sealing is beneficial for preserving the texture and flavor of fermented foods during long-term storage.

Fermented foods can also be preserved using traditional canning methods, such as water bath canning or pressure canning. Canning involves heating the fermented foods to a specific temperature for a certain period to kill any remaining bacteria or yeast and create a vacuum seal that prevents the entry of oxygen and contaminants. Canned fermented foods like pickles, relishes, and chutneys can be kept at a room temperature for extended periods, making them convenient and shelf-stable options for long-term storage. However, it's essential to follow proper canning procedures and guidelines to guarantee the safety as well as quality of the canned foods.

Furthermore, adding natural preservatives such as salt, sugar, vinegar, or alcohol to fermented foods can help prolong their shelf life by preventing the development of spoilage organisms and preventing oxidation. Salt acts as a natural antimicrobial agent, while sugar and vinegar create an acidic environment that inhibits bacterial growth. Additionally, alcohol produced during fermentation can act as a preservative, further extending the shelf life of the fermented foods. By adjusting the salt, sugar, vinegar, or alcohol content of fermented foods, fermenters can tailor the preservation method to suit the specific type of ferment and desired shelf life.

In conclusion, techniques for extending the shelf life of pickled and fermented foods are essential for preserving their quality, flavor, and safety over time. Proper fermentation, storage, packaging, preservation, and the addition of natural preservatives can help ensure that these delicious and nutritious foods remain safe and enjoyable to eat for longer periods. Whether fermenting vegetables, pickling fruits, or canning relishes, understanding and implementing these techniques can help fermenters create delicious and shelf-stable foods that can be enjoyed for months or even years to come. With careful attention to detail and proper preservation methods, pickled and fermented foods can be a valuable addition to any pantry or emergency food supply, providing a reliable source of sustenance and enjoyment in any situation.

## Monitoring Fermented Foods for Spoilage

Monitoring fermented foods for spoilage is crucial in ensuring their safety, quality, and enjoyment. Fermentation is a natural process that involves the development of beneficial microorganisms, such as lactic acid bacteria and yeast, which transform sugars and starches in food into acids, alcohols, and other compounds. While fermentation can help preserve foods and enhance their flavor, monitoring fermented foods carefully to detect any signs of spoilage, contamination, or off-flavors that may indicate microbial growth or other issues is essential. In this section, we will explore the importance of monitoring fermented foods for spoilage, as well as the signs to watch for and the steps to take to ensure the safety and quality of fermented foods.

One of the primary reasons for monitoring fermented foods for spoilage is to ensure their safety for consumption. While fermentation creates an acidic environment that inhibits the growth of harmful bacteria as well as molds, it's still possible for fermented foods to spoil or become contaminated under certain conditions. Factors such as improper fermentation, inadequate sanitation, temperature fluctuations, or exposure to oxygen can increase the risk of spoilage and microbial growth. By monitoring fermented foods regularly, fermenters can detect any signs of spoilage or contamination early and take appropriate action to prevent foodborne illness or other health risks.

Additionally, monitoring fermented foods for spoilage helps ensure their quality and flavor remain intact. Fermented foods should have a characteristic aroma, texture, and taste that reflect the specific type of ferment and the ingredients used. Any changes in aroma, appearance, or flavor may indicate spoilage or contamination and should be investigated further. Common signs of spoilage in fermented foods include off-flavors, mold growth, slimy or mushy texture, or unusual colors or odors. By monitoring fermented foods for these signs, fermenters can keep the quality and integrity of their ferments and ensure a positive culinary experience for themselves and others.

Sensory evaluation is one of the most effective ways to monitor fermented foods for spoilage. Sensory evaluation involves observing and assessing fermented foods' appearance, aroma, texture, and taste to detect any signs of spoilage or contamination. Fermenters should inspect fermented foods regularly for changes in appearance, such as mold growth, discoloration, or separation of liquids. They should also sniff the fermented foods for any off-putting odors or unusual aromas that may indicate spoilage. Additionally, fermenters should taste a small sample of the fermented foods to assess their flavor, acidity, and overall palatability. Any deviations from the expected sensory characteristics may warrant further investigation and corrective action.

In addition to sensory evaluation, fermenters can use pH testing to monitor the acidity of fermented foods. pH testing involves measuring the pH level of the fermented foods using a pH meter or pH test strips. Fermented foods should have a low pH (below 4.6) due to the production of lactic acid during fermentation, which helps prevent the growth of harmful bacteria and molds. Monitoring the pH of fermented foods can help fermenters ensure that the fermentation process is proceeding as expected and that the foods remain safe and stable for consumption. Any significant changes in pH may indicate fermentation problems or spoilage and should be investigated further.

Furthermore, fermenters can use visual cues to monitor the progress of fermentation and detect any signs of spoilage. For example, bubbles or foam on the surface of fermented foods may indicate active fermentation, while a cloudy or murky appearance may indicate microbial growth or contamination. Fermenters should also inspect the fermentation vessel for any signs of gas buildup, such as bulging lids or swollen containers, which may indicate the presence of harmful bacteria or yeast. Any unusual or unexpected changes in appearance should be investigated promptly to prevent spoilage or contamination.

In conclusion, monitoring fermented foods for spoilage is essential for ensuring their safety, quality, and enjoyment. Fermentation is a natural process involving the growth of beneficial microorganisms, transforming sugars and starches in food into acids, alcohols, and other compounds. While fermentation can help preserve foods and enhance their flavor, monitoring fermented foods carefully for any signs of spoilage or contamination is essential. By using sensory evaluation, pH testing, and visual cues, fermenters can detect and prevent spoilage, ensuring their fermented foods remain safe, delicious, and enjoyable. With proper monitoring and attention to detail, fermenters can confidently enjoy the many benefits of homemade fermented foods while minimizing the risk of foodborne illness or other health concerns.

## Rotation Strategies for Maintaining a Constant Supply

Rotation strategies are essential for maintaining a constant supply of pickled and fermented foods, ensuring the diet's freshness, variety, and nutritional balance. Pickling and fermenting are age-old methods of food preservation that have been practiced for centuries to prolonged the shelf life of perishable foods and enhance their flavor and nutritional value. By regularly rotating batches of pickled and fermented foods, individuals can ensure that they always have a steady supply of these delicious as well as nutritious foods on hand, reducing waste and ensuring food security. In this section, we will explore the importance of rotation strategies for pickled and fermented foods, as well as practical tips for putting into practice effective rotation practices.

One of the primary reasons for implementing rotation strategies for pickled and fermented foods is to ensure freshness and quality. Pickled and fermented foods have a limited shelf life, even when properly stored, and can lose their flavor, texture, and nutritional value over time. By regularly rotating batches of pickled and fermented foods, individuals can ensure that they consume them at their peak freshness and flavor, minimizing the risk of spoilage or deterioration. This ensures that each batch of pickled or fermented foods is enjoyed to its fullest potential, maximizing culinary enjoyment and nutritional benefits.

Additionally, rotation strategies help maintain variety and diversity in the diet, as different batches of pickled and fermented foods may have unique flavors, textures, and nutritional profiles. Pickling and fermenting allow individuals to preserve a wide range of fruits, vegetables, and other ingredients, each with its distinctive characteristics and culinary applications. By regularly rotating batches of pickled and fermented foods, individuals can enjoy diverse flavors and textures in their diet, ensuring a well-rounded and balanced nutritional intake. This enhances culinary enjoyment and provides a broader range of nutrients as well as phytochemicals that contribute to overall health and well-being.

Furthermore, rotation strategies help minimize waste and optimize resource utilization by ensuring that pickled and fermented foods are consumed before they spoil or lose their quality. Pickling and fermenting often involve seasonal or abundant harvests of fruits and vegetables, which may need to be preserved in large batches to avoid waste. By regularly rotating batches of pickled and fermented foods, individuals can prioritize consumption of older batches while allowing newer batches to mature and develop flavor. This ensures that all batches of pickled and fermented foods are consumed promptly, minimizing the risk of waste and maximizing the use of available resources.

Practical tips for implementing rotation strategies for pickled and fermented foods include labeling containers with the date of preparation and using a first-in, first-out (FIFO) system to prioritize consumption of older batches. When storing pickled and fermented foods, arrange containers in the pantry, refrigerator, or other storage areas so that older batches are easily accessible and consumed before newer batches. Keep track of inventory levels and plan meals and recipes to ensure that pickled and fermented foods are regularly incorporated into the diet. Additionally, consider sharing excess batches of pickled and fermented foods with friends, family, or neighbors to avoid waste and promote community sharing and food security.

In conclusion, rotation strategies are essential for maintaining a constant supply of pickled and fermented foods, ensuring the diet's freshness, variety, and nutritional balance. By regularly rotating batches of pickled and fermented foods, individuals can enjoy these delicious and nutritious foods at their peak freshness and flavor while minimizing waste and optimizing resource utilization. Practical tips for implementing rotation strategies include labeling containers, using a first-in, first-out system, and planning meals and recipes to incorporate pickled and fermented foods regularly. With proper rotation practices in place, individuals can enjoy a steady supply of pickled and fermented foods year-round, enhancing culinary enjoyment and promoting overall health and well-being.

# CHAPTER X

# Adaptability and Resourcefulness in Pickling and Fermenting

## Using Wild and Foraged Ingredients in Pickling and Fermenting

Using wild and foraged ingredients in pickling and fermenting is a practice deeply rooted in traditional culinary knowledge and a connection to nature. It involves harnessing the flavors and nutrients of wild plants, berries, mushrooms, and other edibles to create unique and flavorful preserves. This age-old practice not only adds diversity and excitement to culinary endeavors but also encourages a deeper appreciation for the natural world and promotes sustainable harvesting practices. Wild and foraged ingredients offer an array of flavors, textures, as well as nutritional benefits that can enhance the complexity and depth of pickled and fermented foods.

One of the key benefits of using wild and foraged ingredients in pickling and fermenting is the opportunity to navigate and celebrate the diversity of natural flavors. Wild herbs such as dandelion greens, nettle leaves, and wild garlic provide a range of tastes from bitter and peppery to savory and pungent. Berries like elderberries, blackberries, and huckleberries offer sweetness and acidity, while mushrooms such as chanterelles, morels, and porcini provide earthy and umami-rich flavors. Incorporating these wild ingredients into pickling and fermenting recipes adds layers of complexity and depth, resulting in preserves that are truly unique and reflective of their natural surroundings.

Moreover, using wild and foraged ingredients in pickling and fermenting fosters a deeper connection to the land and promotes sustainable harvesting practices. Foraging for wild ingredients encourages individuals to explore their local landscapes, learn about native plants and ecosystems, and develop a deeper understanding of seasonal rhythms and cycles. It also promotes responsible harvesting practices, such as only taking what is needed, leaving no trace, and respecting natural habitats and wildlife. By incorporating wild and foraged ingredients into pickling and fermenting recipes, individuals can support biodiversity, preserve traditional knowledge, and foster a sense of connection to the land and community.

However, using wild and foraged ingredients in pickling and fermenting also presents certain challenges and considerations. Foraged ingredients may be seasonal, transient, or limited in availability, requiring individuals to plan and harvest them at the peak of freshness and abundance. Additionally, wild ingredients may require special handling or preparation to remove any dirt, insects, or toxins that could affect the safety as well as the quality of the final product. It's essential to research and properly identify wild plants and mushrooms before foraging and to follow sustainable harvesting practices to minimize impact on natural ecosystems.

Practical considerations for using wild and foraged ingredients in pickling and fermenting include selecting and preparing suitable ingredients for preservation and fermentation. Choose wild ingredients that are fresh, ripe, and free from signs of decay or damage, and wash or clean them thoroughly before use to remove any dirt, insects, or contaminants. Consider experimenting with different combinations of wild and foraged ingredients to create unique flavor profiles and culinary experiences. Additionally, be mindful of any special handling or storage requirements for wild ingredients, such as refrigeration or dehydration, to preserve their freshness and quality.

In conclusion, using wild and foraged ingredients in pickling and fermenting offers a creative and sustainable way to explore the flavors and textures of the natural world. By incorporating wild herbs, berries, mushrooms, and seaweeds into pickling and fermenting recipes, individuals can create preserves that are truly unique, flavorful, and reflective of their local environment and culinary heritage. While challenges and considerations are involved in using wild and foraged ingredients, the rewards are well worth the effort, including a deeper connection to nature, enhanced culinary experiences, and a greater appreciation for the land's bounty. With proper planning, harvesting, and preparation, anyone can enjoy the delights of using wild and foraged ingredients in pickling and fermenting and embark on a delicious journey of exploration and discovery.

## Making the Most of Seasonal Produce

Utilizing seasonal produce in pickling and fermenting preserves the abundance of fresh fruits as well as vegetables and captures the essence of each season's flavors and aromas. Seasonal produce offers many culinary possibilities, with each fruit and vegetable boasting unique characteristics and nutritional benefits. By harnessing the flavors and nutrients of seasonal produce through pickling and fermenting, individuals can enjoy a diverse array of preserved foods year-round while reducing food waste and supporting local agriculture. This section will delve into the significance of utilizing seasonal produce in pickling and fermenting, exploring practical strategies for maximizing flavor and nutritional value while celebrating the bounty of nature's harvest.

The practice of utilizing seasonal produce in pickling and fermenting aligns with traditional food preservation methods and sustainable living principles. In the past, before the advent of modern refrigeration and transportation systems, people relied heavily on seasonal harvests to sustain themselves throughout the year. Pickling and fermenting emerged as effective techniques for preserving surplus fruits and vegetables during times of abundance, ensuring a stable food supply during leaner months. Today, the practice remains relevant as individuals seek to reconnect with nature's rhythms, reduce their environmental footprint, and support local food systems.

One of the main benefits of using seasonal produce in pickling and fermenting is the opportunity to capture the peak flavors and nutritional content of fruits and vegetables when they are at their freshest. Seasonal produce is typically harvested at the height of ripeness, resulting in superior taste, texture, and nutrient density compared to produce that has been picked prematurely or stored for extended periods. By pickling and fermenting seasonal produce at its peak, individuals can preserve these qualities, ensuring they can enjoy the vibrant flavors and health benefits of fresh fruits and vegetables long after the harvest season.

Moreover, utilizing seasonal produce in pickling and fermenting allows individuals to celebrate each season's unique flavors and characteristics. From the delicate sweetness of spring strawberries to the robust earthiness of autumn squash, seasonal produce offers a diverse palette of flavors and textures that can be preserved and enjoyed throughout the year. By embracing the changing seasons and incorporating seasonal ingredients into pickling and fermenting recipes, individuals can create a culinary experience that is both dynamic and reflective of nature's cyclical rhythms.

Additionally, utilizing seasonal produce in pickling and fermenting supports local agriculture and promotes sustainability. Seasonal produce is often sourced from local farmers and growers, reducing the carbon footprint associated with long-distance transportation and storage. Individuals can support their communities by purchasing seasonal produce from local sources, preserving agricultural diversity, and reducing reliance on industrialized food systems. Pickling and fermenting seasonal produce also helps minimize food waste by preserving surplus harvests that may otherwise go unused or unsold, contributing to a more sustainable and resilient food system.

Practical strategies for maximizing seasonal produce's flavor and nutritional value in pickling and fermenting include selecting ripe, fresh ingredients at the peak of their season and experimenting with various flavor combinations and fermentation techniques. Consider incorporating seasonal fruits and vegetables into traditional pickling recipes, such as cucumbers, beets, carrots, and peppers, or experimenting with unconventional ingredients like berries, stone fruits, and leafy greens. Explore different fermentation methods, such as lacto-fermentation, brine fermentation, and vinegar pickling, to achieve desired acidity, flavor, and texture levels.

In conclusion, utilizing seasonal produce in pickling and fermenting offers a delicious and sustainable way to preserve the flavors and bounty of each season. By harnessing the peak freshness and flavor of seasonal fruits and vegetables, individuals can create diverse preserved foods that celebrate the changing seasons and support local agriculture. Practical strategies for maximizing flavor and nutritional value include selecting ripe, fresh ingredients, experimenting with flavor combinations, and exploring various fermentation techniques. With creativity and ingenuity, anyone can harness the flavors of the seasons in their pickles and ferments, creating culinary delights that nourish the body and soul year-round.

## Scaling Recipes for Different Group Sizes

Scaling recipes for different group sizes in pickling and fermenting is a practical and versatile skill that allows individuals to adapt their preservation efforts to meet the needs of various occasions, whether it's a small family meal or a large gathering. Pickling and fermenting have long been valued for their ability to extend the shelf life of perishable foods while enhancing flavor and nutritional value. By understanding how to adjust ingredient quantities, fermentation times, and container sizes, individuals can ensure that their pickled and fermented creations are consistently delicious and well-suited to the size of the group they are serving. In this section, we will explore the importance of scaling recipes for different group sizes in pickling and fermenting and practical tips for adapting recipes to meet specific needs.

One of the primary reasons for scaling recipes in pickling and fermenting is to ensure that the final products are well-balanced and flavorful, regardless of the group size being served. The ratio of ingredients in pickling and fermenting recipes plays a crucial role in achieving the desired taste and texture, and adjusting these ratios for different batch sizes is essential for maintaining consistency and quality. Whether preparing a small batch for personal consumption or a large batch for a social gathering, it's important to carefully calculate ingredient quantities to ensure that the flavors are properly balanced and the fermentation process proceeds smoothly.

Furthermore, scaling recipes allows individuals to optimize resource utilization and minimize waste by producing the appropriate amount of pickled and fermented foods for the occasion. For example, when preparing for a small family meal, making a smaller batch of pickles or ferments may be more practical to avoid leftovers that may go uneaten or spoil. Conversely, when planning for a larger gathering or event, scaling up the recipe can help ensure that there is enough food to go around without excess waste. By adjusting batch sizes to match the group's needs, individuals can reduce food waste, save money, and promote sustainability in their preservation efforts.

Practical tips for scaling recipes for different group sizes in pickling and fermenting include adjusting ingredient quantities proportionally based on the desired batch size and considering factors such as fermentation vessel size and fermentation time when planning the recipe. When scaling up or down, it's essential to maintain the same ratios of ingredients to ensure that the flavors remain balanced and consistent. For example, if a recipe calls for 2 pounds of cucumbers, 1 cup of vinegar, and 1 tablespoon of salt to make pickles for four people, scaling it up to serve eight people would require doubling all the ingredients to maintain the same flavor profile. Similarly, when adjusting fermentation times, consider factors such as temperature, humidity, and ingredient composition to ensure the fermentation process proceeds appropriately.

In addition to adjusting ingredient quantities, individuals may also need to consider the size and type of fermentation vessels used when scaling recipes for different group sizes. Larger batches may require larger containers or multiple containers to accommodate the increased volume of ingredients, while smaller batches may be more suited to smaller jars or containers. Ensuring that the fermentation vessel provides enough space for the ingredients to ferment properly without overflowing or spilling over could lead to contamination or uneven fermentation. Individuals can ensure that their pickled and fermented foods are produced safely and efficiently by selecting the appropriate fermentation vessel for the batch size.

In conclusion, scaling recipes for different group sizes in pickling and fermenting is a valuable skill that allows individuals to adapt their preservation efforts to meet the needs of various occasions. By adjusting ingredient quantities, fermentation times, and container sizes, individuals can ensure that their pickled and fermented creations are well-balanced, flavorful, and suited to the size of the group they are serving. Practical tips for scaling recipes include maintaining proportional ingredient ratios, considering fermentation vessel size, and adjusting fermentation times as needed. With a little planning as well as foresight, anyone can successfully scale recipes for pickling and fermenting and produce delicious preserves for any group size.

## Creative Ways to Utilize Pickled and Fermented Foods in Cooking

Pickled and fermented foods are delicious on their own and versatile ingredients that can add depth, complexity, and tangy flavors to a wide range of dishes. From salads and sandwiches into stir-fries and tacos, there are countless creative ways to incorporate pickled and fermented foods into cooking, elevating dishes to new heights of flavor and sophistication. In this section, we will explore some innovative and inspiring ways to utilize pickled and fermented foods in cooking, highlighting their versatility, nutritional benefits, and culinary potential.

One creative way to use pickled and fermented foods in cooking is to incorporate them into salads and grain bowls. Adding pickled vegetables such as cucumbers, carrots, and radishes to salads can provide a burst of acidity and crunch, while fermented foods like sauerkraut and kimchi add depth of flavor and probiotic benefits. Pickled and fermented vegetables can also be used as a topping for grain bowls, adding texture and complexity to dishes made with grains such as quinoa, rice, or bulgur.

Consider experimenting with different combinations of pickled and fermented ingredients to create unique and vibrant salads and grain bowls that are both nutritious and satisfying.

Another creative way to use pickled and fermented foods in cooking is to incorporate them into sandwiches and wraps. Adding pickled vegetables such as onions, peppers, and jalapenos to sandwiches can provide a tangy contrast to savory fillings like roasted meats, cheese, and spreads. Fermented foods like kimchi and pickled cabbage can also add a spicy kick and probiotic benefits to sandwiches and wraps. Consider layering pickled and fermented ingredients between slices of bread or wrapping them in tortillas or lettuce leaves for a flavorful and satisfying meal on the go.

Pickled and fermented foods can also be used to add depth as well as complexity to stir-fries and noodle dishes. Adding pickled vegetables such as mushrooms, bamboo shoots, and water chestnuts to stir-fries can provide a tangy and savory flavor boost, while fermented foods like miso and soy sauce add umami richness and depth. Pickled and fermented ingredients can also be used to create flavorful marinades and sauces for stir-fries and noodle dishes, adding complexity and depth of flavor to dishes made with vegetables, tofu, meat, or seafood. Consider experimenting with different combinations of pickled and fermented ingredients to create unique and flavorful stir-fries and noodle dishes that are sure to impress.

In addition to savory dishes, pickled and fermented foods can also be used to add flavor and complexity to sweet dishes and desserts. Adding pickled fruits such as cherries, peaches, and figs to desserts like cakes, tarts, and ice cream can provide a tangy and sweet contrast to rich and creamy flavors. Fermented ingredients like yogurt and kefir can also be used to add tanginess and probiotic benefits to desserts like smoothies, parfaits, and frozen treats. Consider experimenting with different combinations of pickled and fermented ingredients to create unique and delicious sweet dishes and desserts that are sure to delight your taste buds.

In conclusion, pickled and fermented foods are versatile ingredients that add depth, complexity, and tangy flavors to various dishes. From salads and sandwiches to stir-fries and desserts, there are countless creative ways to incorporate pickled and fermented foods into cooking, elevating dishes to new heights of flavor and sophistication. Whether you're aiming to add a tangy kick to your salads, sandwiches, or stir-fries, or to experiment with unique flavor combinations in your sweet dishes and desserts, pickled and fermented foods offer endless possibilities for culinary creativity. So why not get creative in the kitchen and start experimenting with pickled and fermented foods today? Your taste buds will thank you!

# CONCLUSION

As we come to the close of our journey through "A Tactical Cookbook for Preppers: Ancient Methods for Modern Survival," we reflect not only on the practical knowledge gained but also on the more profound lessons learned about resilience, adaptability, and the enduring power of tradition. Throughout these pages, we have explored the age-old practices of pickling and fermenting, uncovering their timeless relevance in the modern world and their potential to transform our food and lives.

At its core, this book has celebrated self-reliance and preparedness, reminding us that in the face of uncertainty, there is strength in knowledge and sustenance in tradition. Through the art of pickling and fermenting, we have discovered a pathway to resilience, harnessing the transformative power of beneficial bacteria and enzymes to preserve our foods and nourish our bodies in even the most challenging circumstances.

But beyond the practicalities of food preservation, we have also explored the broader implications of pickling and fermenting, discovering how these ancient practices can foster community, connection, and a deeper appreciation for the natural world. From sharing recipes and techniques to cultivating beneficial microbial cultures, we have seen how food can serve as a catalyst for establishing relationships and forging bonds that transcend boundaries and borders.

As we look to the future, the lessons of pickling and fermenting offer us a roadmap to sustainability and resilience in an increasingly uncertain world. In an era of climate change, economic instability, and global pandemics, the need for self-sufficiency and preparedness has never been more apparent. By embracing the wisdom of our ancestors and learning to harness the power of pickling and fermenting, we can equip ourselves with the skills and knowledge needed to thrive in the face of adversity.

But perhaps most importantly, the journey through this book has reminded us of the importance of resilience in the human spirit. In every recipe and technique, we have seen evidence of our capacity to adapt, innovate, and overcome even the most daunting challenges. From the humble beginnings of preserving foods for long journeys to the sophisticated art of crafting gourmet ferments, we have witnessed the indomitable spirit of humanity shining through.

As we bid farewell to these pages, let us carry forward the lessons learned as well as the knowledge gained, knowing that the power to shape our destiny lies in our hands. Whether we are seasoned preppers or curious novices, let us continue to explore, experiment, and embrace the timeless wisdom of pickling and fermenting as we journey through the ever-changing landscape of the modern world.

In closing, let us remember that the journey towards self-sufficiency and resilience is not solitary but a shared endeavor that binds us together as a community. So let us stand together, united in our pursuit of a brighter, more sustainable future, as we continue to learn, grow, and thrive in the face of whatever challenges may come our way.

*Thank you for buying and reading/ listening to our book. If you found this book useful/ helpful please take a few minutes and leave a review on the platform where you purchased our book. Your feedback matters greatly to us.*